Dear England

James Graham

T0021354

methuen | drama

LONDON • NEW YORK • OXFORD • NEW DELHI • SYDNEY

METHUEN DRAMA
Bloomsbury Publishing Plc
50 Bedford Square, London, WC1B 3DP, UK
1385 Broadway, New York, NY 10018, USA
29 Earlsfort Terrace, Dublin 2, Ireland

BLOOMSBURY, METHUEN DRAMA and the Methuen
Drama logo are trademarks of Bloomsbury Publishing Plc

First published in Great Britain 2023

Photography by Rick Guest and CGI by Rob Rae.
Art direction and graphic design by
National Theatre Graphic Design Studio.

A catalogue record for this book is available from the British Library.

A catalog record for this book is available from the Library of Congress.

ISBN: PB: 978-1-3504-3529-2
ePDF: 978-1-3504-3531-5
eBook: 978-1-3504-3530-8

Series: Modern Plays

Typeset by Mark Heslington Ltd, Scarborough, North Yorkshire
Printed and bound in Great Britain

To find out more about our authors and books visit
www.bloomsbury.com and sign up for our newsletters.

Dear England had its world premiere at the National Theatre's Olivier Theatre on 20 June 2023 with the following cast and production team:

Jordan Pickford **Josh Barrow**
Gary Lineker/Sven-Göran Eriksson/Boris Johnson/Wayne Rooney **Gunnar Cauthery**
Harry Kane **Will Close**
Alex Scott/Roxanne/Theresa May **Crystal Condie**
Gareth Southgate **Joseph Fiennes**
Jordan Henderson **Will Fletcher**
Sam Allardyce/Fabio Capello/Panama Manager/Physio Phil **Sean Gilder**
Bukayo Saka **Ebenezer Gyau**
Marcus Rashford **Darragh Hand**
Greg Clarke/Gianni Infantino/Matt Le Tissier **John Hodgkinson**
Harry Maguire **Adam Hugill**
Jadon Sancho/Kieran Trippier **Albert Magashi**
Raheem Sterling **Kel Matsena**
Pippa Grange **Gina McKee**
Dele Alli **Lewis Shepherd**
Mike Webster **Paul Thornley**
Greg Dyke/Steve Holland/Graham Taylor **Tony Turner**
Eric Dier **Ryan Whittle**
Ensemble **Nick Barclay, Tashinga Bepete, Bill Caple, Will Harrison-Wallace and Miranda Heath**

Other parts played by members of the company

With huge thanks to Abdul Sessay

UNDERSTUDIES
Jordan Pickford/Jordan Henderson/Harry Maguire/Eric Dier **Bill Caple**
Gary Lineker/Sven-Göran Eriksson/Greg Clarke/Gianni Infantino/Matt Le Tissier/Fabio Capello/Panama Manager/Mike Webster **Nick Barclay**
Boris Johnson/Sam Allardyce/Physio Phil/Greg Dyke/Steve Holland/Graham Taylor **Will Harrison-Wallace**

Wayne Rooney/Harry Kane **Ryan Whittle**
Alex Scott/Roxanne/Pippa Grange **Miranda Heath**
Gareth Southgate **Will Fletcher**
Bukayo Saka/Marcus Rashford/Raheem Sterling **Tashinga Bepete**
Jadon Sancho **Lewis Shepherd**
Dele Alli **Albert Magashi**

Director **Rupert Goold**
Set Designer **Es Devlin**
Costume Designer **Evie Gurney**
Lighting Designer **Jon Clark**
Co-Movement Directors **Ellen Kane and Hannes Langolf**
Co-Sound Designers **Dan Balfour and Tom Gibbons**
Additional Music **Max Perryment**
Video Designer **Ash J. Woodward**
Casting **Bryony Jarvis-Taylor**
Dialect Coach **Richard Ryder**
Company Voice Work **Cathleen McCarron and Shereen Ibrahim**
Associate Director **Elin Schofield**
Associate Set Designer **Will Brown**
Associate Lighting Designer **Ben Jacobs**

Producer **Rachel Quinney**
Production Manager **Anthony Newton**
Dramaturg **Nina Steiger**
Stage Manager **Ian Farmery**
Deputy Stage Manager **Fran O'Donnell**
Assistant Stage Managers **Ellie Leaver and Edie Fitt-Martin**
Deputy Production Manager **Mekel Edwards**
Movement Captain **Kel Matsena**
Project Draughting **Tom Atkinson and Jef Gage**
Digital Art **Daniel Radley-Bennett**
Costume Supervisor **Tash Prynne**
Assistant Costume Supervisor **Sydney Florence**
Wigs, Hair & Make-up Supervisor **Philip Carson-Sheard**
Running Wardrobe Supervisor **Ruth Williams**
Prop Supervisor **Matilde Marangoni**

Dear England transferred to the Prince Edward Theatre in London's West End on 9 October 2023 with the following cast and production team:

Bukayo Saka **Denzel Baidoo**
Jordan Pickford **Josh Barrow**
Gary Lineker/Sven-Göran Eriksson/Boris Johnson/Wayne Rooney **Gunnar Cauthery**
Harry Kane **Will Close**
Alex Scott/Roxanne/Theresa May/Sarina Weigman/Liz Truss **Crystal Condie**
Gareth Southgate **Joseph Fiennes**
Jordan Henderson **Will Fletcher**
Marcus Rashford **Darragh Hand**
Greg Clarke/Gianni Infantino/Matt Le Tissier **John Hodgkinson**
Sam Allardyce/Fabio Capello/Panama Manager/Physio Phil **Lloyd Hutchinson**
Pippa Grange **Dervla Kirwan**
Jadon Sancho/Kieran Trippier **Albert Magashi**
Raheem Sterling **Kel Matsena**
Dele Alli **Lewis Shepherd**
Harry Maguire **Griffin Stevens**
Mike Webster **Paul Thornley**
Greg Dyke/Steve Holland/Graham Taylor **Tony Turner**
Eric Dier **Ryan Whittle**
Ensemble **Nick Barclay, Tashinga Bepete, Kate Kelly Flood, Will Harrison-Wallace, Miranda Heath, Tom Mahy and Tristan Waterson**

Other parts played by members of the company.

UNDERSTUDIES
Jordan Pickford/Jordan Henderson/Harry Maguire/Eric Dier **Tom Mahy**
Gary Lineker/Sven-Göran Eriksson/Greg Clarke/Gianni Infantino/Matt Le Tissier/Fabio Capello/Panama Manager/Mike Webster **Nick Barclay**

Boris Johnson/Sam Allardyce/Physio Phil/Greg Dyke/Steve Holland/Graham Taylor **Will Harrison-Wallace**
Jadon Sancho/Kieran Trippier/Dele Alli **Tristan Waterson**
Wayne Rooney/Harry Kane **Ryan Whittle**
Alex Scott/Roxanne/Pippa Grange/Theresa May **Miranda Heath**
Liz Truss/Sarina Wiegman **Kate Kelly Flood**
Gareth Southgate **Will Fletcher**
Bukayo Saka/Marcus Rashford/Raheem Sterling **Tashinga Bepete**

Director **Rupert Goold**
Set Designer **Es Devlin**
Costume Designer **Evie Gurney**
Lighting Designer **Jon Clark**
Co-Movement Directors **Ellen Kane and Hannes Langolf**
Co-Sound Designers **Dan Balfour and Tom Gibbons**
Video Designer **Ash J Woodward**
Additional Music **Max Perryment**
Casting Director **Bryony Jarvis-Taylor**
Dialect Coach **Richard Ryder**
Company Voice Work **Cathleen McCarron**
Associate Director **Elin Schofield**
Associate Set Designers **Benjamin Lucraft and Will Brown**
Associate Lighting Designer **Ben Jacobs**
Associate Sound Designer **Alex Twiselton**
Resident Director **Rasheka Christie-Carter**
Movement Captain **Kel Matsena**
Production Manager **Paul Hennessy**
Costume Supervisor **Cáit Canavan**
Wigs, Hair & Make-Up Supervisor **Philip Carson-Sheard**
General Manager **New Road Theatricals**

Dear England

Characters

Gareth Southgate, *England football manager, forty-six to fifty-two years old*
Pippa Grange, *sports psychologist, also forty-six to fifty-two*

The rest are played by a rotating ensemble:

McNulty, *reporter*
Roe, *reporter*
Sam Allardyce, *former England manager*
Greg Clarke, *FA chairman*
Greg Dyke, *outgoing FA chairman*
Roxanne, *FA head of operations*
Graham Taylor, *former England manager*
Sven-Göran Eriksson, *former England manager*
Fabio Capello, *former England manager*
Theresa May, *prime minister*
Mike Webster, *team analyst*
Steve Holland, *assistant coach*
Physio Phil, *physio*
Alex Scott, *presenter*
Gary Lineker, *presenter*
Panama Manager, *coach*
Matt Le Tissier, *pundit*
Boris Johnson, *prime minister*
Liz Truss, *prime minister*
Sarina Wiegman, *England women's football manager*
Gianni Infantino, *FIFA president*

Players

Harry Maguire	**Raheem Sterling**
Dele Alli	**Eric Dyer**
Bukayo Saka	**Jordan Henderson**
Harry Kane	**Kieran Trippier**
Wayne Rooney	**Jadon Sancho**
Jordan Pickford	**Chloe Kelly**
Marcus Rashford	

Reporters/Commentators/Players/Staff/Fans/Kids

Setting

The play takes between June 2016 and December 2022, although it will jump back to past moments over sixty years of football . . .

It takes place in multiple locations that don't have to be literally realised, the majority of these being the St George's Park training ground, the FA offices, and the dressing rooms and pitches of stadiums around the world.

Prologue

Against the darkness, we hear the building sounds of a stadium full of England **Fans** *in full voice. The inevitable chanted singing of* 'It's coming home' . . .

We hear the commentary of Brian Moore echoing around us . . .

A whistle sounds, as the lights begin to slowly fade up . . .

We see that we're at Wembley.

For now – the twin towers loom over the space . . .

A colosseum, surrounded by the sound and sight of 70,000 fans, and the St George's Cross waving . . . There's a sole figure, lonely in grey. His hands around his neck in despair.

Brian Moore   '. . . A mild evening, here at Wembley. Filled with noise and with high emotion.'

This lone figure is **Gareth Southgate**. *Standing alone at the penalty spot . . .*

Brian Moore   'So we go into sudden death penalties. Recently forced his way into the England side, Southgate. Does everything right.'

'Let's hope he can do this right as well.'

'. . . Saved it! And the Germans go into the final, and England are out.'

'The dream is over for England . . .'

Suddenly, there is silence.

And only the sound of **Gareth**, *breathing heavily . . .*

Act One

Scene One

Twenty years later.

Outside the Football Association.

Two reporters – **McNulty** *already here,* **Roe** *arriving – getting their gear together, pads, recorders.*

Roe Here we go again, then! Shit the bed. Where is he? Big Sam? He arrived?

McNulty He's inside. They have (*dramatically*) 'summoned him in'.

Roe Bloody hell. I mean is that a record, then? One game!

McNulty Shit, he's coming out –

Sam Allardyce, *the current England manager, marches out of the FA, in a big coat and chewing gum.*

He's full of northern energy and speaks at a lick, as the **Press** *surround him in a gaggle.*

McNulty/Roe/Press Sam?! / What was the meeting about?! / You been sacked?!

Sam Allardyce No, I have not been sacked, ta very much. Nevertheless, I would like to make a short statement. And that's to say that, though I have not been sacked, right . . . it has been mutually agreed that I shall be 'voluntarily resigning', with immediate effect.

Roe So do you admit wrongdoing?

Sam Allardyce Look, it seems that I was secretly filmed by one of your lot – cheers by the way – giving some bad financial advice about player transfers and, yes, I was a bloody fool to say some of the things I said in what I thought was a private dinner.

McNulty   Is it painful, Sam, it must hurt –

Sam Allardyce   Ey. I grew up in Dudley. I know pain.
Right. But yeah, course it hurts. Very sad – dream job – gone
after one game – there you are. I wish my successor, whoever
it may be – and God help 'em – the very best.

Right. That's on the record. Off the record, now? Yes? Phil?
Len? . . . Off the friggin' record, you lot have stabbed me in
my heart, honest to God you have.

Roe/McNulty   Aw, come on / How's that, then?

Sam Allardyce   No-no, you all spent years saying, 'Get Big
Sam in', 'Give Sam the top job' – and then what do you do? I
were brought in because we lost to bloody Iceland – Iceland!
A tiny volcanic rock! There's more folk what *shop* in frozen
foods Iceland than bloody live there! And now look, me –
opportunity wasted.

McNulty   To be fair, you were caught saying some choice
words about your predecessors, and over a pint of wine,
Sam. That's a bit –

Sam Allardyce   So what? See that's the problem with you
lot, you don't understand that's what English people *want* in
a manager. England manager – pint of wine.

He heads off, as the **Press** *pack follows like a murmuration, twisting
around the space – flash, flash –*

Sam Allardyce   You wanna write summat? (*Tapping
someone's pad.*) Yeah, I only had one game. But I won it,
didn't I? 100 per cent winning record, me. Write *that* down.

He heads off apace, the pack in pursuit with more questions.

Inside the FA – the chairman's office.

Gareth Southgate *steps tentatively in, as the current chairman*
Greg Clarke *and the outgoing chairman* **Greg Dyke** *fight fires
– phones ringing.*

Gareth   Hello, morning, I uh –

Greg Clarke   Ah, Gareth! Come in, come in. Sorry to drag you here at such a frenzy. It's nice to properly meet, I mean I know we've – over the – but . . . (*Shaking.*) Greg Clarke, new chairman, hello.

Gareth   Hi, Greg. Gareth.

Greg Clarke   And you probably know the *outgoing* chairman, Greg Dyke.

Greg Dyke   You don't have to be called Greg to run the FA, but it helps. (*Laughs; they shake.*)

Gareth   Greg.

Greg Dyke   I'm basically not here. Pretend I am not here. I am just a sort of interim bit of continuity as we transition. This is his ship, he's the captain. Maiden voyage.

Gareth   Right. (*Then, joking.*) 'Iceberg, iceberg.' Hah.

Greg Clarke   'Iceberg'?

Gareth   Nothing. Anyway, dear oh dear, poor Sam.

Greg Clarke   Yeah. Poor Sam. But. How you getting on, with the under-21s?

Gareth   Yeah, yes, the new pathway, it's starting to bear real fruit, some really special players coming through.

Greg Clarke   Well, you obviously know why you're here. We need someone to man the fort, while we look for a permanent replacement for Sam.

Gareth   . . . Oh. Ok, I see –

Greg Dyke   Of which – if it's not me overstepping, Greg – you'd be also in the running for, obviously.

Greg Clarke   Oh, no of course. Exactly.

Gareth   Right. Thank you. Although, just to say it out loud, no modern caretaker manager has ever gone on to actually *be* . . . the manager, have they, so. But –

Greg Dyke   But, you know, you never know, you know. So . . .

Greg Clarke   We're not expecting the world, let alone the World *Cup*, but some sense of *turning* a corner would be nice.

Greg Dyke   And *scoring* from a few would be even better. Hah.

Greg Clarke   Russia's just round the corner. So, if you'd be happy to step in, during the qualifiers . . .

Gareth   Well. That's very flattering, to be asked. Really.

Greg Dyke   And shit scary, too. (*Laughter.*) We get it. 'The Impossible Job.' As they say. And I ran the fucking BBC, so I know about national institutions and pleasing nobody all of the time.

Greg Clarke   And regarding all that, actually. The 'pressure'. What's your feelings now about . . . your experience of England, since playing. Your own history, I suppose, is defined – for a lot of people, not us necessarily, but . . . is defined by a particular –

Gareth   My penalty, against Germany.

Greg Clarke   I – . . . exactly. Yes, and, bravo for just – hah, for just coming out and saying – . . . 'Hello, Mr Elephant, I didn't see you there.' Hah, I –

Gareth   Er, so look. Greg?

Greg Clarke/Greg Dyke   Yes?

Greg Clarke   Oh, / sorry, I didn't –

Greg Dyke   No-no, it's ok, you –

Gareth   I would obviously only be able to manage the team, even for a short time, in the way I would want to do it. And work on the things I think need to be done.

Greg Clarke   Course, yeah. And . . . what do you think needs to be done?

Gareth   . . . I think we have a problem.

A short moment.

Greg Clarke   Well, yes. That's why we're here. Our results –

Gareth   I mean something bigger. I mean . . . I think something, erm . . . I think there's something really wrong. Guys.

Greg Clarke   . . . Could you be a little more specific?

Gareth   I don't know, I wish I knew. I just know that – I *sense* that, for us to be where we are, right now, for it to feel how it feels . . . that something has gone wrong, in, England.

How we can have all this talent, this history, be the home of the sport, the biggest leagues, and yet . . . look at us.

We're – 'stuck'. Doesn't it feel like we're, like, stuck? Unable to, to – move on, move forward?

And, and it's about more than just a series of – setbacks. More than tactics, talent, technique. I think – . . . I think we *all* have a problem, with what it is to be England, at the moment . . .

And, I wish I knew what it was and how to fix it, I do. All I know is I don't think that sticking plasters will cut it, anymore; it's about asking some probably, maybe, uncomfortable questions about . . . almost everything. About how we run, and manage, and play, and think about, and feel about . . . English football, itself.

A moment. **Greg Dyke** *eventually sighs, rubbing his face.*

Greg Dyke   Fuck's sake, ok. Erm . . . Gareth. Look. I get it.

Gareth   I hope that's not –

Greg Dyke   No-no-no, course. All that stuff. Thirty years of hurt, forty, fifty. I get it –

Greg Clarke   I think that, for right now, opening up a big old can of worms . . . when we're looking to just find some stability, right now. The nearest port in the storm, which is why you're, we think, perfect. For now.

Pause. **Gareth** *nods.*

Gareth   I agree. About stability.

Greg Clarke   . . . Good. Well! Welcome. Current England manager.

Polite smiles. **Gareth** *nods, and leaves. The* **Gregs** *look at one another.*

Greg Dyke   What the fuck have we done?

Scene Two

A cross-section of **Fans** *appear – who'll be a recurrent chorus throughout. Traditional English roles and professions, but in the modern world.*

Pub Drinker   Hold up, hold up, Southgate?

Barber   Gareth Southgate, really?

NHS Nurse   Oh yeahhh, Southgate, yeah.

Pub Drinker   The guy who – fuck me. The guy who – Jeeesus!

Deliveroo Rider   Give him a chance! No one gets given a chance.

Fish and Chip Shop Owner   That's not even scraping the barrel, that's scraping *through* the barrel, breaking the barrel into pieces, tossing those pieces into a skip, finding some shit in the skip and scraping that!

Entertainer   Oh, give it a rest; fuckin' bullies! Doing my head in. I know 'little shits', believe me, and Gareth is no shit, he's sweet; a sweet guy.

Lollipop Man   Yeah but do we want a 'sweet guy'?

Snooker Player   'Ooh, he's such a *nice boy*, isn't he, our Gareth.'

Lollipop Man   I went to school with so many 'Gareths'. And they were all – they were just all such fucking '*Gareths*', you know?

Snooker Player (*in a nerdy voice*)   'Hello, I'm Gareth, would you like to share my cheese sandwich.'

As we find – a **YouTuber** *for a 'Fan TV' channel, speaking to* **Fans** *with a roving mic.*

YouTuber   Yo, don't forget to click like and subscribe; as ever we are touring the terraces, picking up the pulse of the people. So – you a big England fan?

Shy Builder   Uh, yeah.

YouTube   What's your advice to Gareth on winning a trophy?

Shy Builder   Uh. Invent a time machine? That would help. (*Laughs.*)

Louder Fan (*grabbing the mic*)   What's everyone talking about? He was a CLINICAL defender, man! He captained Palace, he captained Middlesborough!

Vicar   I still struggle to forgive him.

YouTuber   Dude, twenty years ago!

Vicar   I know, I know.

YouTuber   Spread the word!

As these **Fans** *all morph into –*

The **Press** *pack, moving like a flock again to –*

Press   Gareth! / Gareth! / Gareth!

Gareth *is led into the media suite by* **Roxanne**, *head of operations.*

Roxanne   Morning, everyone. Before questions, Gareth would like to say a few words.

Gareth   . . . Yeah, just really to say, erm, I realise the last week has been a very difficult one, for our organisation. But the reason I'm here, is, I always feel it's important to step forward into a leadership position, when asked. I'm aware that I'm standing on the shoulders, of – a great many giants . . .

Some of the **Press** *somehow morph and snap into – the previous managers.*

Roxanne   – Mr Graham Taylor.

Roe   Graham, any comment on this drunken bender the team had during training?

Graham Taylor   I knew it, see, straight in with the negativity. They each had – to wind down, they had a few drinks, in a couple of nightclubs –

Roe   We've confirmed it was eleven clubs, Graham –

Graham Taylor   They had a few drinks, in *eleven* nightclubs. *Why* always so negative, so miserable. Do I not like that!

Put smiles on your faces. That's it . . . Fuckin' hell!

I love you all, really.

Snaps, transforming into –

Roxanne   Sven? A few words?

Sven-Göran Eriksson   Uh, well.

I should say thank you. Although, standing here – this feels like some sort of hostage situation. Please, send the ransom. Ahah.

But no. England manager is, still, the biggest job in all world football.

I know I am the first foreign manager you have had. I know not everyone is happy. But maybe – change is good.

Snap, into –

Fabio Capello *speaking in fluent Italian, which* **Roxanne** *translates over the top of.*

Roxanne   'I know it is very important for me to learn English, and I am taking lessons every day. You gave the world Shakespeare; us, the Enlightenment. Together, I believe a new Renaissance can be born here in the home of the game.'

'But only with discipline. Regulation. Hard work. We are not here to have – fun.'

And snap, back into –

Gareth   And I very much look forward to working in the coming days to get the results the country wants. Which is to qualify for the next World Cup.

Ok, questions, uh –

Press (*hands in the air*)   Gareth! / Gareth! / Gareth!

. . . Prime minister?!

A flash from the cameras, as **Roxanne** *transforms into –*

Theresa May   I'm grateful to have been appointed as leader, and – therefore – prime minister. I am aware this wasn't expected. But now it's time to focus on delivering the Brexit that people voted for, and most importantly bringing the country back together again. It's within our own hands, now . . . to decide who, and what, we want to be. Thank you.

Gareth *and* **Theresa May** *glance at one another, before stepping away, as we move into –*

A meeting room.

Where **Gareth** *is being introduced to the senior coaching staff.*

Mike   Alright, gaffer, pleasure to, etcetera. Mike Webster.

Gareth   Of course, hi, Mike. Uh . . . this is uh, Steve –

Mike (*hand out to*)   Steve Holland, yeah course. Your reputation, and so on. Real pleasure.

Steve Holland *offers his hand – an imposing presence and a man of few words.*

Steve   Hello, Mike. How's it going?

Gareth   I . . . (*Awkwardly.*) Look, I know you were assistant manager, under Sam . . . It's only that . . . Steve has been my own number two for a –

Mike   Look, it's not my first rodeo, ok. We're all grown-ups. I'm here, so let's just – let's see how it plays out, alright?

(*Then.*) This is Phil. – 'Physio Phil'.

Physio Phil   How do, how do, alright? How was the firing squad? Press conference?

Gareth   They were fine, fine. As expected. They come with an idea of 'you', you know, and try and make that image stick.

Physio Phil   Oh yeah, what, 'Oh is he tough enough?', 'Oh, is he too nice?' That bollocks.

Gareth   Exactly, yeah, that bollocks.

Then . . .

Uh, I bought some, er, some muffins, for everyone, if . . .

Mike   Oh, lovely, that, that's very sweet of you, Gareth.

Physio Phil   Do you know what actually, not for me, gotta set an example for the – ooh, is that an *almond* croissant though, ah shit, ok I'll just tear off a tiny – actually fuck it then, touched it now, may as well have the whole –

As pastries are shared, coffee poured, etc. **Gareth** *paces, trying to find his stride.*

Gareth   And, look, I get that as a caretaker . . . it's hard to make any real impact. But . . . if I could set out just one or two of my main goals – apart from goals, hah . . . then I suppose it would be . . . well, look, simply put, it's to – get people smiling again.

Mike   . . . Sorry, boss, get people –?

Gareth   Uh, smiling, get them smiling again.

Mike   Oh. Oh, right.

Gareth   I want England to make those watching happy, and you happy. Again.

The past, five–six years, this team has had what many feel was a golden generation of players – Gerrard, Lampard, Rooney, Beckham. And yet at the same time we've had a series of our worst results almost ever, so – how can that be? We're not – we're not *seeing* something.

Do you know – erm, you know space?

Mike   Space?

Gareth   Yeah, 'space'. Sun, moon, stars. Before black holes were discovered, they didn't know why things behaved the way that they did, they just knew that objects were bending around *something*, some great unseeable Thing affecting the behaviour of the universe.

So. 'What can't we see', what's going wrong? Honestly. It's safe to say anything here.

Mike   . . . Well, ok, so the clubs don't help. The players get smoke blown up their arse, paid millions. Then they come to

England camp, get asked to play for free and take a load of shit from the fucking press.

Steve   I will say . . . at Chelsea, when we sent players here – it's like we're 'lending' them to you. And you'd better send 'em back how you found them – no injuries, no 'new ideas'.

Physio Phil   Ok, I'll say it. They're arrogant. The players.

Mike   Yep, some of 'em, yes.

Gareth   Well –

Physio Phil   No, look, cause I have 'em on my table, right, as physio – you get these privileged insights. And this generation of players, Gareth, swear down? A lot of them don't want to be here. They tell me. A lot of them try to get out of it. 'Get out of it'! England!

Gareth   Ok, well . . . that's huge, isn't it? Aren't we asking why, why that is?

Mike   I don't think it's quite as bad as – I wouldn't say that –

Physio Phil   Because they're spoilt! That's what. Imagine that on the beaches of Normandy. 'Ooh sorry General Montgomery, I don't really fancy this today, do you mind?'

Gareth   OK, alright, thanks Phil –

Physio Phil   'Do mind ringing up Hitler, can you ask Hitler to postpone it today, I'm not in quite the right frame of mind.' Fucking hell!

Get 'em to turn up, work hard. No more photo shoots. No more haircuts. No more WAGS! You show up with passion, you perform, or you piss off.

A moment. He sticks the last bit of croissant in his mouth.

There. I'm sorry but you did ask.

Gareth   Ok, but uh . . . good, ok. Good start.

. . . I wonder, though, if we should also be looking . . . 'within'.

Mike   Within?

Gareth   You know, we've gone the technical route, the past decade, improved that – and we're worse than ever. So, it might be helpful to get some – *different* new people in, to help, with this. Starting with a . . . a psychologist, maybe.

Mike   . . . (*Teasing.*) Pressure getting to you already, is it?

Gareth   For the players. Mike. I – I don't think the problem is just out there on the pitch, I think it's here. (*Taps his head.*)

Mike   Yeah, ok, so the lads . . . traditionally, you know they don't love someone watching them, trying to analyse their every move. They might have more and more of that fluff at club level, but we only get snatches of a player's time and they don't tend to want to spend it on a therapist's couch.

Gareth   And that's why we need the right person. If we could begin that search.

We find –

Through the audience, or the swirling projected images of a presentation, comes – **Pippa Grange***, speaking calmly, and intimately, through a handheld mic.*

Pippa   When was the last time you were scared?

Yes. 'Scared', I am using the word scared. In a room full of adults, I know. Deep breath. And just – think about it.

The last time you were overwhelmed by such waves of worry, anxiety.

Smiles now, as she relaxes the room.

Don't get me wrong, some fear is necessary, of course. But it can force us to make poor decisions. As people, institutions . . . countries, even. If it comes from a place of panic, frustration, resentment.

For me, the real tragedy of fear – if we don't use our power to harness it – is not what it *does* to us. It's what it *takes*. It robs us of potential joy. The job we didn't apply for. Not telling that person how we feel . . .

So much of the modern world now is actually geared around helping us escape decision-making. That's why there's this feeling right now – isn't there? Of 'paralysis', everywhere?

As 'leaders', then . . . how do you cultivate an environment that isn't stale. That isn't full of fear. By helping your team *confront* their fears. And that starts . . . by confronting your own.

Thank you.

Snap to –

Gareth   Doctor Pippa Grange?

Pippa   Oh. 'Gareth Southgate'.

Gareth   Hah. Gareth's fine without the Southgate, hi.

Pippa   Well, Pippa's fine, without the Doctor. Hello. Uh, are we – did we –?

Gareth   Yeah, sorry, I hope this doesn't feel like an ambush or a tackle from behind at ten yards. I know we've been calling, trying to . . . I'm just a fan of your work.

Pippa   Huh, well. Now I really feel bad declining your interview – thank you. It's just – I don't think it's for me, I'm sorry.

Gareth   I get it. I sort of think that's why we think it *is* for you, huh.

I know that football hasn't always been as welcoming to, to psychologists, as other sports –

Pippa   I *was* a performance psychologist, now I'm more of a – 'culture coach'. Not focused on individual performance, so much. More transforming the whole culture of a place.

Gareth   . . . Ok. Well. That's exactly why I'm here, Pippa.

I've been put in a car already going at 100 mph whose entire engine I want to change but I'm already driving it, so I need changemakers, from the outside. If we get through qualifiers, if I survive, I plan to build a new team, new people. For, a New England.

And I suppose also, to say it out loud, as a woman you'd –

Pippa   That bit I'm used to, believe me, being the sole female in teams of men. Although the England changing room, I mean . . . Jesus, I can only imagine –

Gareth   And you'd be right. You'd be bang on. There's a lot about this game I don't like or agree with, Pippa. It's – it can be stubborn, cruel. But what can I say, I love it.

Pippa   Ok. And what are you asking help for, then? Brass tacks.

Gareth   . . . I'd settle, right now, for the team feeling better. They're not in a good way, they're . . . (*Referencing her.*) Doctor, doctor, they're not very well. Hah.

The pressure they face – they're not handling it. It's . . . all the things I think you know about . . .

Pippa   And *you* know about. Right? What *you* went through.

A moment, **Gareth** *not necessarily having expected to go 'here'.*

Gareth   Well. Exactly. And I don't want any of these young men to go through that.

Pippa   I am sorry, that must have been, just, huge. All those years ago.

Gareth   Honestly, thanks, but, it's Ok. I'm Ok.

I am. I-I-I actually am. And I know by saying 'I-I-I' three times, it makes it sound like I'm not, but . . .

Pippa (*studying him, a small smile*)   Hmm.

Gareth   'Hmm', is that a good 'hmm', or?

Pippa   . . . 'England', you say.

Gareth   Yeah. Yeah, come help fix England with me.

Pippa   . . . Can I think about it?

Gareth   . . . Yeah. Of course.

She leaves him, as **Gareth** *instead joins –*

Steve, *getting ready to go 'club to club', selecting their players.*

Steve   Well?

Gareth   Come on, we don't stop now. 'In with the new.'

Steve   Player selection. How brave are you feeling?

Gareth   Let's build from the back. 'Defence'. My old position . . .

To – the Leicester City dressing room/club insignia.

Harry Maguire   No! Seriously?! Mr – Gareth, uh, sir. Southgate – 'Sir Southgate', that's not right. Wait. You were – you were watching *me*?

Steve   We were, yeah.

Gareth   Impressive, Harry. You're developing into a strong centre-back.

Harry Maguire   . . . Oh well, ta. Ey it – it's what us Yorkshire lads are known for, ey. Strength! Grr. You've moved up there, right, is that right?

Gareth   Yeah, yeah. Harrogate.

Harry Maguire   I'm Sheffield.

Gareth   Nice. Only a stone's throw, right, it's what, an hour down the A1?

Harry Maguire   . . . I mean, honestly I'd avoid the A1 if I were you, boss, better to go A61 down to Shadwell, change onto the A6120 –

– and then circle back onto the M1 straight down to junction 34.

Gareth You're right, I don't know what I was thinking – but, see? You've a strong head, for things, Harry.

Harry Maguire Oh aye. (*Slaps it.*) Just get me near that ball and bam!

Gareth I meant – your character. I'm looking for 'character'. And you have it . . .

A moment – they shake – **Gareth** *and* **Steve** *exiting. Alone,* **Harry Maguire** *shakes his fists in unrepressed joy.*

Before – as with all these sequences – we (could) have a brief movement motif, as the **Player** *demonstrates their 'style' of play, abstractly, in the transition.*

Steve Clean passes. A strong anchor. Good in the air . . .

Gareth (*nods, then . . .*) Midfield.

Tottenham Hotspur dressing room.

Dele Alli *ready to leave – shades already on, jacket on. He whips them all off when he sees his visitors.*

Gareth Dele, hey.

Dele Alli Hellooo, boss, hi, Steve – look, I know I was off form today –

Gareth It's ok, it's alright.

Dele Alli And that fucking wanker ref, man – sorry, I didn't mean to say fucking.

Gareth Or wanker.

Dele Alli No that one I meant. Um. But, for real, I just wanted to say thank you, for this chance, I *know* it's a chance –

Gareth Hey, Dele, I've been watching you through our development programme. You can go anywhere, push forward, drop back, score! The great all-rounder. *We're lucky. Ok?*

Into – **Dele***'s brief sequence, as he departs.*

Gareth (*watching*)   Powerful. Aggressive. Fast . . . unpredictable?

Steve   Maybe we need a bit of that.

Into –

The England under-19s – 'Young Lions'.

Bukayo Saka*, eating a Twix, with a book.*

Gareth   Bukayo . . .

Bukayo Saka   Oh my gosh, boss! Sorry, I'm eating a Twix. Steve, I have been following the diet plan, I just . . .

Steve   Yeah, well, you'd better be. But – just this once.

Bukayo Saka   One of these and my Bible, they'd be my, like, two desert island things, you know.

Gareth (*at the Bible*)   Wow. That's great, Bukayo. What's your favourite, you know, 'bit'?

Bukayo Saka   I would say the biscuit, man, probably; gives it crunch –

Gareth   I meant the Bible.

Bukayo Saka   Ohhh! I see. I don't know, it's all good. It all reminds me that God is there, guiding me. That he has a plan.

Gareth   Well. He's not the only one. Bukayo. I want to get you training with the seniors. You are the future, after all.

Bukayo Saka   . . . 'The future'. Wow. Thanks, boss.

And he spins off –

Gareth (*watching*)   Creative. Explosive. Hungry . . .

As finally, we're into –

Tottenham Hotspur again.

Harry Kane   Oh, hello, coach. Hi, Steve. Hi, how are you, both?

Steve   How are *you*, Harry. Jesus, a hat-trick.

Harry Kane   Uh, yeah, yeah that was nice. Pleased about that. For the lads, you know.

Gareth   It's like you can score from anywhere, Harry. And any foot!

Harry Kane   Oh. Thanks, yeah I'm better on my right. But. I don't mind my left, you know. Left or right, right or left Mainly those two. Huh. But –

Gareth   Well, England is excited to see what you're capable of, Harry.

Nods – shakes – off he goes.

Gareth   One of the best finishers we've seen for a generation . . . He's my number 9.

Steve   Yeah. Except of course . . . you already have a Number 9.

A moment, as they step into –

The England dressing room, finally.

Wayne Rooney, *shirt on, getting ready for training – boots, pads.*

Wayne Rooney   Alright, boss?

Gareth   Wayne. How you feeling? I'm sorry, about all the speculation in the media about – your 'future', and . . .

Wayne Rooney   Always the way innit, to be expected. And it's great, you know, all these new kids coming up. I look at a lot of 'em, and I'm like, wow. Great.

Gareth   . . . Good. Yeah. I suppose . . . I've got some ideas of what I think we might need to do, here, to seize this moment with . . . exactly, some newer, younger . . .

Wayne *is starting to get it. Studying* **Gareth**.

Wayne Rooney   Ahuh. Right. Yeah . . .

Gareth *can't quite (yet) seem to say the words. So, in an act of generosity,* **Wayne** *helps him out.*

Wayne Rooney   It's like the Scouse me ma makes.

(*Off* **Gareth***'s look.*) The Stew?

Wayne Rooney   Everyone has their own recipe like, thinking theirs is boss, but my ma's *was* better, and that's because everyone else puts way too much Worcester sauce in it, too many other spices. But having competing flavours doesn't make the best taste, does it. It's about a *balance*. And my ma understood that, and I understand that.

Gareth *nods.*

Gareth   Fifty-three goals, for England, Wayne. The most ever.

Wayne Rooney   No silverware to show for it though, ey.

Wayne *takes his executioner in. A strange shift in status.*

Wayne Rooney   . . . Little Gareth, ey. The 'Gate'. Swinging in the wind . . . Alright.

Wayne *heads towards a 'tunnel', into some light – a recurring motif for those characters who exit our story.*

As we hear commentary building up to –

Commentary   . . . 'England versus Slovenia then, and our last chance to qualify.

The chorus of **Fan** *return, to drums – and chants – and flags.*

YouTuber   So here we are, back at Agony Central then, the 94th minute, still 0–0.

Loud Fan   Why?! Why do we *do* this to ourselves, every time! Whhyyyyyyy?!

Party Clown   Whistle's about to blow, this is our last chance!

Fish and Chip Shop Owner   Reminds me of David Beckham, free kick, dying seconds, against Greece.

NHS Nurse   Yeah well, I'd quite like my dying seconds to be up against David Beckham in grease.

Suddenly they all point at the screen in excitement –

All   Ooh!!!!!!

Then – cheers!

Fans   Ye-es!

YouTuber   . . . The 94th minute, though. Dudes, seriously . . . again . . .

As the sign is displayed –

Commentary   'England are going to Russia . . .'

Scene Three

St George's Park emerges properly now.

The new 'home' of England. Its training and development centre. Someone arrives to slowly raise the England flag up a flagpole . . **Pippa Grange** *is arriving, stopped by . . .*

Security Guard   Oh sorry, miss, you can't go through there.

Pippa   Oh, it's ok I . . . (*Shows her pass.*) . . . I work here, now. Apparently, which I'm still getting used to as a concept, but –

Security Guard   Women's team facilities, they're the other side of the courtyard.

Pippa   Oh. Ok. I'm actually *with* the men's team, though, which is – through there, I think, isn't it? (*Reading his badge.*) Mark?

Security Guard   Yeah but – there's men, like, getting changed in there, you know. The players and coaching staff, it's –

Pippa   Is there a place for me to get changed then, as a woman, *in* the men's team?

Security Guard   Uh . . . I'll be honest, I'm struggling to square that.

Pippa   Ok.

Into –

Gareth *and his senior coaching* **Team** *are passing through on the way to the first day of training –* **Mike, Physio Phil** *and* **Steve,** *as* **Greg Clarke** *intercepts.*

Greg Clarke   And behold! The new 'permanent' England manager! All hail!

His fellow **Team** *cheer and clap.*

Greg Clarke   Well, as permanent as England manager gets. Mob-dependent, and all that, haha. Good luck, anyway! First full day of training for Russia!

Gareth   Thank you, Greg, that's –

Greg *just briefly leads* **Gareth** *off, privately –*

Greg Clarke   Although, just to 'spade a spade' it . . . we did only scrape through, and, the whole Rooney decision, you know. That's – hah. That's, for the fans, what with ticket sales down, shirt sales, that's –

Gareth *sees* **Pippa Grange** *arriving, interrupting this.*

Gareth   Greg, I should – Pippa? You – you *are* here. I wasn't sure if –

Pippa   Yes, I'm sorry. I had one last little, uh . . . but yes. I'm here. If you still –

Gareth   Yes. Yes, we 'still'. Everyone, this is Doctor Pippa Grange, joining our team.

Others   Hey / Hi / Hello.

Gareth   She'll be focusing a lot on our – psychological 'resilience'.

Greg Clarke   . . . Right. A doctor, right. 'Our' being the players, presumably. (*Laughing*.) Not us, here.

Pippa   . . . Uh, well – no, I – forgive me, not to dive straight in, but I think it, it's work that everyone, in a team, has to embrace, for it to take hold, so . . .

A moment.

Mike   Well, let's go and do some actual football, shall we?

As people disperse, a brief moment with **Pippa** *from* **Gareth**.

Gareth   Thank you . . .

New **Players** *we haven't met yet step into a light/turn to a 'camera' and pose as though being introduced in the 'line-up' on TV before a match – their name and stats in graphics.*

Jordan Pickford   Jordan Pickford. Everton.

Marcus Rashford   Marcus Rashford. Man U.

Raheem Sterling   Raheem Sterling. Man City.

Eric Dier   Eric Dier. Spurs.

Jordan Henderson   Jordan Henderson. Liverpool

Kieran Trippier   Kieran Trippier. Spurs.

Joined by **Harry Kane**, **Harry Maguire** *and* **Dele Alli**.

Dele Alli   Dele Alli. Spurs.

Harry Maguire   Harry Maguire. Leicester City.

Harry Kane   Harry Kane. Spurs.

They split off from one another at pace – stretching, exercising. Young men – rivals in normal time – getting the measure of one another.

Dele Alli   Yeah, where we at, where we at?

Marcus Rashford   Dele. Yo! Behind!

Dele Alli *ignores him, passing to* **Harry Kane.** *Teasing –*

Dele Alli   Ah sorry, Marcus, I didn't hear you, you've got to speak up, have more confidence, bro.

Marcus Rashford   Uh, excuse me, who scored more goals this year? Hmm, lemme think.

Jordan Henderson   Ouch.

Raheem Sterling   Pff, not ouch, 'Hendo'. As if. I say this with proper modesty, but uhhhh who got named 'player of the month' this month? Oh lemme think, lemme think.

Harry Kane   Aw, that's awesome, Raheem, well done.

Jordan Pickford   A'right, Harry.

(*For the others' benefit – at* **Harry Kane.**) This here's the only one of yous to get a ball past me at Everton this year, so, you know, respect to the Harry Kane. We are not worthy and all that.

Dele Alli   You're Jordan, right?

Jordan Pickford   Yeah, Jordan, you know my name, Dele, I know you do.

Dele Alli   I'm just checking cause, like, you're from the same place as *that* 'Jordan', right (*At* **Jordan Henderson.**)

Jordan Pickford   Uh, ay, yeah. Sunderland, ay.

Dele Alli   So what, d'you have to be called Jordan to come from Sunderland? (*Laughs.*) Did you go to the same school, were you best mates?

Jordan Pickford   Nah.

Jordan Henderson   Uh, no. Nah-no. And we have two Harrys.

Harry Maguire   Not from the same exact fucking street though, or whatever.

Jordan Henderson   And how are *you*, Eric; how's the injury? You know, groin strain.

Eric Dier   Wasn't an injury, Hendo, just a little 'twinge' that's all. Why you asking?

Jordan Henderson   What, I'm just asking, sensitive.

Eric Dier (*smiling, knowingly*)   Right, yeah, you're just 'asking'.

Jordan Henderson   I am, being nice!

Eric Dier   I just think it's interesting you're so interested in my groin all of a sudden, you don't think that's a bit –

Jordan Henderson   Ok, so piss off.

Gareth *arrives with his coaching staff –* **Pippa** *included.*

Mike   Alright, you horrible lot, look alive. Welcome to your first day back here training at St George's! And here is the boss – attention, captain on deck!

Some applause and 'yehhs' to welcome **Gareth**, *officially.*

Gareth   Thank you. Morning. You know a lot of these guys already. But one our newest members of the backroom staff here is . . . Dr Pippa Grange. Our head of People and Team Development.

Raheem Sterling   'Head of People'. What, she's head of *all* the people?

Gareth   No, she's a – psychologist.

Pippa   Hi, everyone.

Some shift in the room. **Players** *are never sure about this.*

Gareth   We work on training our bodies. So, we're also going to be working a lot on what's going on upstairs, as well as downstairs.

Dele Alli   I don't really have an upstairs, I'm like a bungalow.

Gareth   You have a great upstairs, Dele, nice and spacious, lovely views. Well, first things first. Wayne is stepping back from the team.

A reaction.

Jordan Pickford   Ah, man, no way, I always – it's been my dream, to like, play with –

Gareth   I know. And just to give you . . . like Mike said. Some stirring rhetoric. For the campaign ahead . . . And . . . well, and you're just about the greenest team England will have ever put out on the pitch. And I'm saying that as a really good thing. Because I want to say, uh . . .

A moment. As he works up to saying what he's about to say . . .

Look. Look. We are probably not going to win the World Cup.

A moment. The other staff splutter. **Mike** *in mild panic, nervous laughing . . .*

Mike   I – ha, I think – that's very funny. I think what the boss means is . . . actually I don't know what the boss means.

Gareth   No, I know, I just want to alleviate you of that expectation. That burden. We really probably are not going to win this World Cup.

Physio Phil (*head in his hands*)   Jesus Christ.

Gareth   And the good news is – no one else expects
anything of us either, and why should they? Why do we
believe that England can and should win, every time? On
what evidence? Over the past say sixty years? Where have
we come?

Yes, in 1966 – yes, at home – we won. Brilliant. But after
that? 1970 – we came eighth. 1974 – we didn't even qualify.

1978 – we didn't qualify. Then we came 6th. Then 8th. Then
4th. 9th. 6th. 7th. Then 13th. And most recently – 26th!

But in the press, on the terraces, in the pub, in here, every
time? 'We better come first, better win, this is our time, don't
fuck it up.'

Raheem Stirling   Isn't it just about having belief, though –

Jordan Henderson   Exactly, if we don't think we can win
then why are we here?

Gareth *might glance towards* **Pippa** *briefly here, in a supporting
role still, for now.*

Gareth   . . .It's about relieving ourselves, of impossible
expectations. And facing our truth.

So we can 'create', uninhibited. Like a ballet dancer would a
dance move. Or a writer, a story.

Jordan Pickford   Ballet dancer.

Gareth   Yeah, why not. I am going to use that word a lot.
'Stories'. England needs – a new story. And, *we*, together . . .
are going to write one.

You know what a story is?

He writes on a flip chart.

A three-act structure? Beginning, middle and end? The
great, classic stories of old. Shakespeare, opera?

. . . Or like *Star Wars.*

Players   Oh yeah, *Star Wars* / Yeah, banging / Ok / Princess Leia would get it.

Gareth   Right, so, what's the set-up for the beginning of *Star Wars*?

Harry Maguire   Well, which trilogy: the original, the prequels or the sequels, cause they're very, very different. Sorry, I'm too excited, I need to chill . . .

Harry Kane   Luke gets the gang together and they destroy the Death Star.

Gareth   Right, that's the set-up, then ok, Act Two? Act Three?

Harry Maguire   Luke trains to become a Jedi.

Harry Kane   He resists the temptation to go over to the dark side, and, he makes up with his dad. It's nice.

Gareth   – and everyone lives happily ever after, end of story. One – two – three. That's a *good* story.

England's problem. We're always starting here. (*Underlines 'Act Three'.*) Everyone want us to be there already. Because we have all these old stories, about being the Best, being First, that we've absorbed and are trying to recycle, and retell. Because we had one bloody good day in 1966, when no one in this room was even born.

So, we are going to write our own history. Our own story. Which is going to take time.

He reveals a digital clock. Counting down.

Marcus Rashford   Oh my God, it's like a bomb.

Gareth   It's not a bomb –

Jordan Henderson   . . . So what's happening in six years, five months, twenty-one days and nine hours?

Gareth   That's the World Cup final, in Qatar. 2022.

That's Act Three. Act One – Russia World Cup. Act Two – Euro 2020. Act Three – Qatar. And hopefully – the happy ending, to our story. *That's* what we're aiming to win.

So we can just – breathe. Ok? Breath.

Takes in the room.

We're all storytellers now, gentlemen. And we're going to take our time with it.

Some acknowledgement in the room – if still vaguely sceptical.

Ok. Pippa?

Pippa *steps forward, carefully.*

Pippa   So, to help with some of that . . .

I'm available to you, one on one, as and when. But I also want to plant the idea of what it might feel like to talk openly together, sometimes. Collectively, as an actual – *team*.

To share, some of the things you'll all naturally be feeling, as we face up to the big task ahead. Your worries, or, doubts. Concerns?

She waits, not giving in. Nothing.

Eric Dier   'Awkward silence',

Dele Alli   . . . Ok, uh. Well. I don't think *I* want to talk about 'doubts', though. I don't want that in my head. It's about being positive, innit.

Pippa   No, I get that, I hear that. But . . . if it's something we could think about.

She waits, not giving in. Nothing.

Eric Dier   'Awkward silence'.

Jordan Henderson   Eric. Don't be rude, man; taking the piss.

Eric Dier   Oh what, are you 'sharing', Hendo, *you're* not saying anything neither.

Steve   Lads, settle down, Ok.

Eric Dier   I do think this is bollocks, sorry. Can't we just fucking go train?

Mike   That's not a bad idea –

Harry Maguire   I mean, I'll give anything a go, just . . . sharing *what*? Like –?

Raheem Sterling   Nah, can I just say, I don't like, need to invite you all into my head, my negative thoughts, Ok. I handle them my way.

Pippa   Good. Ok. It's only that . . . when you go out there to play, you need to trust each other, that's all. Which means . . . maybe knowing each other, a little better.

Deli Alli   It just means being focused, committing. What's this 'doubts' bullshit? I'm sorry –

Raheem Sterling   Aw . . . is Dele scared of his feelings?

Dele Alli   Yo, FUCK OFF, Raheem! How's about that for 'feelings', bro?

Gareth   Whoa-whoa, Ok –

Eric Dier   Raheem –

Raheem Sterling   Yes, Eric?

Gareth   Ok –

Marcus Rashford   It's just 'positive mental attitude' innit, that's what she's saying.

Eric Dier   Well, Raheem's got the 'mental' bit and the 'attitude' bit, down at least, so –

Raheem Sterling   Yeah, KEEP PUSHING, Eric, I swear! –

Mike   Hey!

He starts pushing his way over, other **Players** *having to split them apart.*

Steve (*loud*)   ABSOLUTELY NOT! Ok. Not that, not here. Right?!

A quiet descends – as whenever **Steve** *is forced to raise his voice.*

Gareth   Ok. Everyone . . . you're ok. We're all finding our feet. Mike? Steve?

Mike   You and you (**Eric** *and* **Raheem**), take five, everyone else, outside.

The rest begin to leave. **Pippa** *and* **Gareth** *alone.*

Pippa   . . . Well that went well.

Gareth   We give it time. These aren't waters they've been asked to wade into before. Players and the staff.

Pippa   . . . And what about you? If you don't mind me asking. As their leader, what waters are you not keen to swim out into?

Gareth   . . . I think you know.

He turns, determined, stepping into –

The biometrics centre.

The senior coaching **Team**, *including now* **Pippa**.

Bam! images of classic penalties. Maybe videos – or instead movement from our real **Players** *performing classic penalties of old, as though being replayed and replayed on the software.*

Arrows and lines and stats exploding everywhere . . .

Physio Phil   Whoa! Penalties?

Gareth   . . . Penalties. Yup.

Physio Phil   I mean, *you* sure, *given* – and a lot of us are ever so, you know, superstitious of even – I mean I can't even watch 'em, I turn my back and look away, no thank you.

Gareth   Well. They do exist, though. And what I'm learning, is that often, England's had a tendency to avoid difficult, uncomfortable things. Whereas if we all started to call them out more, with kindness and care, of course. But – call 'em out nonetheless.

England – are the very worst in the world, at penalties.

Physio Phil   Right but, no, we can't be the *worst* worst, surely?

Gareth   Yup. We've *never* won a penalty shootout, in the World Cup, not once. And it's increasingly the way that we exit tournaments, in pai – . . .

Well, in the most cruel, and the most painful of ways . . . Thank you, Mike.

Mike   And, on the boss's orders, we commissioned a study to look at it.

Projecting on screen/or in reality with our **Players**.

Steve   So. England lost on penalties . . . in 1990 against Germany, In '98, against Argentina. Against Portugal, in 2004. Against Portugal *again*, fucking hell, in 2006. We lost against Italy, in 2012.

And not forgetting . . . 1996, on home turf. Of course . . .

A brief flicker of **Young Gareth***, on the spot, arms around his neck . . . Our* **Gareth** *watching, not saying anything . . .*

Mike   We're going to look at one of our most painful misses, World Cup 2006. Jamie Carragher's pen.

We find – Jamie Carragher, a memory somewhere. Playing this out . . . standing on the spot . . .

Mike   Jamie does what every player taking a penalty has to do. After two hours of brutal physical play only to reach a draw. Carragher is called up, and takes the long, lonely walk . . .

Away from his teammates. To the spot. Tens of thousands of eyes on him in the stadium. Hundreds of millions watching worldwide. A nation's happiness on his shoulders.

Physio Phil   I hate it, I hate it, I *fucking* hate it . . .

Mike   But *he* is alone. A small figure, on a huge stage.

He places the ball – takes his steps back. He turns, begins his run forward – strikes it well – bottom right-hand corner – it's in! – an eruption in the stands! But shit-fuck-bollocks! Ref has disallowed it. He went *before* the whistle blew, the absolute willy. Nightmare, this. He has to take it again.

A brand new decision almost no player has ever had to make before, and he has to make it fast. 'Do I shoot the same fucking way, is that what the keeper expects, or a *different* fucking way, is *that* what he expects I expect he expects me to do? Shit-shit-shit . . .'

We see this play out, again.

He turns, runs, shoots – aiming the other way – and the keeper saves it. England are out of the tournament on penalties once again.

He took it so fast, it was disallowed.

A table comes up – England at the top.

Look. England take their penalties the quickest, in the world.

An average of 2.8 seconds between whistle and kick. And the Germans? The best in the world. They take three times that. Three times longer, before they shoot! English men go so fast, we're basically the premature ejaculaters of penalties. Sorry to –

Gareth   Ok, I get your point.

Steve   So . . . Good. We have to drill it into their heads to go slower. Gather themselves.

Pippa   But why?

They look at her.

Mike   You what, sorry?

Pippa   Why are they going so fast, sorry? What's making them rush?

Mike   It's not possible to measure 'why'. It just 'is' the case. And . . . forgive me, how is *your* penalty taking, by the way, can I ask?

Pippa   Me? I probably couldn't take one to save my life.

Mike   Ah-uh. Well, so, respectfully, and I do mean respectfully, doctor, but when it comes to decisions around –

Gareth   I know, Mike. Pippa knows that, training and coaching is yours and Steve's department, but on this one thing . . . psychologically . . . Pippa?

Pippa (*looking at the data, at Carragher*)   Our players, like Jamie – look – I'm guessing they more often than not turn *away* from the goalkeeper, when they're stepping back for their run-up, instead of facing them?

They avoid looking at the ball, and the keeper. Their own teammates? Head down? I mean, it's literally what Gareth was describing. 'Avoidance'.

Not looking at the Thing that *scares* them. Guys, the problem is *fear* . . . They're afraid . . .

Mike   Of course they are. It's pens.

Pippa   Around what a penalty represents. For any of us. Making a decision and getting it wrong. Losing people's respect, getting shamed because of it –

Mike   Ah-uh, right-ok, but, this is just football, Pippa, not –

Pippa   Mike, come on, this is *men*. Dealing or not dealing with *fear*. Look at what they do with their own bodies, when they miss?

We cycle through some images of penalties of old – those **Players**
having missed; those **Players** *watching.*

Pippa   They make themselves small. Bring in their arms to
their chest, or their neck, crouching. Like a foetus. Like
children.

I know they look and sound like they're ok, but that's a
deflection. They're afraid. They're carrying around the
trauma of a story we're not helping them to understand –

Mike   'Trau –', they're not – . . . how can they have trauma
for something they weren't there for?

Pippa   Collective trauma is real, it can get passed down,
through people, it – it sits, in a place, in its walls. Its streets.
It can pass through . . . well, the 'soul' . . .

Physio Phil   You believe a football team has a soul, Mike?

Mike   Couple of arseholes, maybe.

Pippa (*smiles – ok. One last go*)   . . . What did you say, Mike?
When they walk up to that spot. (*She does it herself.*) They feel
completely alone. They don't know how to ask for help and
we don't know how to offer it.

Physio Phil   And ok to say it out loud, but – it's *luck*, end of
the day, isn't it? We could spend all this time and, and
headspace thinking you can change it but end of the day, the
keeper dives the right way, that's it! In the lap of the gods,
paper–scissors–stone, toss of a coin –

Gareth   . . . Steve.

Steve (*considers this, shrugs*)   Past managers have chose not to
practise them. So. We practise, train, improve technique,
give ourselves the best shot at taking the best shots.

Gareth   . . . Ok. Ok, this doesn't have to be war between
one way, or the other. Let's devote time to the analytical side.
And to mental preparation as well. Ok?

Mike   But with limited time, how *much* time –

Steve   He's the boss. Mike.

Mike   . . . No, yeah, course. You're the boss, boss.

Mike, **Steve** *and* **Phil** *shuffle off together.*

Pippa   It's going to have to come from you, Gareth. You know that.

Gareth (*younger*)   Left, right, up, down. Hard, soft.

Do you think there's an alternative world where I picked a different spot? Where *that* England is a happier and more confident place as a result.

Pippa   Dunno. Maybe. But we don't live in that England do we, we live in this one. The one where you fucking missed.

It gets a laugh from him, cutting through the atmosphere. And then he almost breaks, as a result, wobbling . . .

Pippa   If you don't 'go there', *they* never will.

Scene Four

Dressing room, back with the **Players**.

Gareth   . . . Ok, so like. My thing . . . that I'd like to share. Comes from what happened, when I played for England, in '96 . . .

It was our biggest game in, like, thirty years. We were hosting the tournament, and everyone in the country was so – happy. There were parties, people were smiling . . .

We were against Germany. Of course. After extra time, it was 1–1, which meant . . . penalties.

All the other players before me, they all scored theirs, the first five. And Germany theirs. So it was sudden death. The first player to miss – their team was out. And there was a silence, in our huddle, 'Who's gonna go next'? Eyes of all England upon us. So I just – put my hand up.

And so I began that walk . . .

But all I was thinking about was what might go *wrong*. What if I tripped, scuffed the ball. My legs were so weak. The whistle went. My head, full of the fog of negativity, and other voices . . . I ran up, kicked the ball softly, like – hah, so so soft. And the keeper rolled gently towards it.

And I just wanted to disappear. I can't tell you . . . I knew I was responsible for ending millions of people's dream.

No one knew what to say to me, in the changing room, and I didn't want them to say anything anyway, I couldn't bear it.

I remember the pictures on TV of people *fighting*, smashing up city centres, rioting against police, in Trafalgar Square. Because of me . . .

The next day I avoided everybody – people who loved me. I couldn't look at them. And I wasn't offered any help. Mental health wasn't really . . . you know, back then.

It was a really, a very bad time. It just was. It nearly stopped me from saying yes to this job. Is the truth. Because I'm afraid of hurting people again, and hurting myself.

But I'm here. I haven't let those fears stop me doing what I love. So. There.

A moment.

Harry Kane   . . . Erm. Wow . . . Like. Wow. Sorry.

Gareth   Thank you.

So . . . what we asked before. Making yourselves available to one another. Create a group, volunteers who can just – 'be there', for each other. For chats, and check-ins; doesn't have to come through us. If anyone thinks they can do that.

Harry Kane   . . . Um, I'm happy to give that a go, yeah.

Jordan Henderson   Uh, sure, I'm – yes, boss.

Gareth   And that's another thing, I know it's tradition, but I no longer want to be called 'boss'. Or 'sir'. Or 'gaffer'. I know, but we're not at school or in the army, and it's infantilising on you. I'm Gareth. Hi, Harry.

Harry Maguire   . . . Hi, Gareth. Ooooh, it's a bit weird.

Gareth   . . . Pippa?

Pippa   Great. Eye-rolling at the ready, but, I'd like you *all* to keep – a journal.

Raheem Sterling   No-o-o. Stop it, cringe.

Pippa   Just in case you ever want to explore any of those thoughts, rattling around in your head. Emotional energy is 'fluid', it needs to move through you, so – help it out.

Gareth   And finally, of course, you need – a captain. As the standard bearer for the new values we're pursuing.

He's holding out the black arm band.

Gareth   The new England captain. Harry Kane.

Some acknowledgement of this from the other **Players**, *though not universal.*

Harry Maguire   Yes, go on, H, get in.

Steve   'Oh, captain, my captain!' Nice one, Harry.

Harry Kane   Thank you, yeah thanks. Try – I'll try not to let you down . . .

Mike (*clapping*)   Ok, let's get out there, come on.

Pippa   You okay?

Harry Kane   Cheers. Yeah. Just taking it all in, but yeah. It's big this, innit.

The **Players** *exit with* **Steve**. **Mike** *and* **Gareth** *alone briefly.*

Mike   Well, there you go. He's – a 'good' lad, good choice. Just . . . well, typically the captain is someone with a bit of

– swagger. Able to rally the team, the fans. And . . . I mean, you've basically picked yourself, Gareth. (*A friendly laugh.*) Which is fine.

Gareth   I . . . I don't see that. Harry's – he's a centre-forward.

Mike   I just don't think he's got the bottle for it.

Gareth   Well, what bigger confidence boost than this, ey

Mike (*hands up*)   Ok. Ok. I'm excited, I am. Onwards!

He goes. **Gareth** *briefly alone, before stepping into the next phase of his mission –*

The canteen.

Players *and* **Suits** *and* **Coaches** *at separate tables.* **Gareth** *stands on a chair, calling out –*

Gareth   People of England, listen up!

Players, it has been decided, no longer will you be allowed to just sit in your 'clubs'.

Players   Oh what / Fuck / Noooo.

Gareth   Look at you – City, United, Arsenal, Spurs. You – are – *England,* now. A team. Musical chairs, up on your feet please, move!

They do, as –

Also! The wider staff here at St George's – players, look around at them, staff, wave hello.

Staff   Hello.

Gareth   We're putting an end to this weird thing where they eat *after* the players. We now all eat *together*. You are here because you're the best at what you do. Well, they are the best at what *they* do. All of them, storytellers in our new story.

Look – you have some of the Lionesses here with you now, see? Alex Scott!

Alex Scott   Uh . . . hey?

Gareth   And some Young Lions. Eddie. Bukayo!

Bukayo Saka   . . . Hello.

Gareth   We are one England. An equal England. Thank you!

He hops down, greeting –

Alex Scott   'One, equal England'? I suppose stranger things, and all that. You know . . . it's not a whinge, but, we still have to hang around waiting at the end of the day, for the lads to finish, before we're allowed on the pitch.

Gareth   . . . I do know that now. Thank you, Alex.

A brief flash of some training drills – it's hard, and fast. Then, afterwards –

The training pitch.

Mike   Good session, lads! Now that you're all knackered, as knackered as you would be after a full ninety minutes, plus extra time . . . *now* is when we'll practise – bah-bah-bam – penalties.

A universal groan. **Steve** *gestures* **Jordan Pickford** *to the goal.*

Steve   Jordan? Ready?

Jordan Pickford *psyching himself up, heading to goal.*

Jordan Pickford   Alright, come on, Pickers! Come ON! You're all over this, man.

Steve   Before each match, we'll be memorising the stats on every opposition player, their most likely placement, preferred foot. And Jordan will have memorised *all* of them, won't you Jordan?

Jordan Pickford Yes, I will have done, yes.

Mike Now, as much as possible in training, we want to replicate the 'environment' you'd face in a tournament. Which means, stupid as it sounds . . . we want you to walk. Do the walk.

Gareth Harry? If you would. All the way back there, with your team?

Harry Kane *goes back again.*

Gareth And now, walk. Feeling the eyes of the world on you.

He does – walking to the spot.

Mike Very good. Excellent walking, Harry.

Gareth Before anything else, Jordan, when the opposing player has taken their shot at you, I want you to pick up the ball, and hand it over to your teammate who's shooting next.

Harry, don't fetch the ball yourself. You're going to wait for Jordan to hand it to you. Jordan.

Jordan Pickford, *smirking a little, walks the ball over to* **Harry Kane**, *handing it to him.*

Gareth There, and have a moment. You are connected, a team.

Jordan Pickford Here you go, Harry.

Harry Kane Thank you, Jordan.

Jordan Pickford And how are you, Harry?

Harry Kane I'm ok, Jordan, how are you?

Gareth Ok, alright –

Jordan Pickford (*fake crying*) I love you, Harry.

Harry Kane (*hugging him, fake crying*) Aw, Jordan, thank you, you too!

Gareth   Yeahhh, great, ok. Pippa?

Pippa   Now, even if Harry misses, what's the worst that could happen?

Mike   I mean try *not* to miss, obviously –

Pippa   Right, but, the answer is, your world won't end because when you turn around –

Gareth   Your teammates aren't going to drop to the ground in anger, ignore you. They're going to come up to you and look at you and hold you and appreciate you.

Jordan Henderson   We APPRECIATE you, Harry!

Pippa   Great, so. What are you feeling, Harry, stood there. Your central nervous system will be starting to send a message to your heart to start pumping faster.

Hand on **Harry Kane***'s heart.*

Pippa   Ga-gun. Ga-gun.

Harry Kane   Uh yeah. Yeah, I feel that.

Pippa   What you *can* do is breathe. That's something you *can* control. Everyone?

A deep breath from everyone.

Pippa   Ok, Now, fear drops your IQ by about 15 per cent, so this is actually the worst time to be making decisions.

Gareth   So? – don't. Make your choice in training, of where to place the ball. Practise that, and stick to it.

And, well, unlike a certain someone a certain number of years ago, he put *his* hand up . . . because there was no plan. We, however, will decide in advance who are takers will be, in what order. And so we'll all know. And it won't change. So . . . breathe. Again.

Everyone takes another deep breath.

Then, as some inflatable beach balls come flying in –

Raheem Sterling   Running bomb!

Training morphs into a 'joy sequence' of silly penalty taking with beach balls.

And – in the 'hydrotherapy pool' (or equivalent), we're re-enacting the images of 2018. The **Players** *mucking about on unicorn inflatables.*

Mike   'Fun'?

Gareth   Yeah. God forbid, Mike. Fun.

Greg Clarke *passing . . .*

Greg Clarke   Great work, Gareth – exciting. 'Culture'. 'Philosophies'!

Before **Greg** *collars* **Mike,** *privately.*

Greg Clarke   Mike, what the fuck's all this we're hearing on the top floor? 'Fail in order to win', 'share your doubts', fucking 'feelings'?

Mike *lifts his arms – 'Don't ask me' – into –*

The briefing room.

Raheem *is reading some 'homework' they were assigned, in his journal . . .*

Raheem Sterling   So, I was given Harry, and . . . (*Clears his throat to read.*) Well, 'The thing about Harry Maguire is that, as everyone knows, he has one of the biggest slab heads, in the known universe.'

Harry Maguire (*sighs*)   Yep, great, right.

Raheem Sterling   'I literally do not understand how he can stand up. Or, like, how when he jumps, it doesn't affect, like, the gravitational pull of the earth.'

Gareth   Ok, Raheem –

Raheem Sterling   'And yet, somehow, he is one of the best defenders we have. Probably *because* of his big slab head. I am glad he is at the back. Because. Basically. He has our backs.'

He sits down.

Gareth   Ok, not – not 'bad', but we do want you to move beyond just taking the piss.

Eric Dier   I mean . . . look. Something I've been . . .

Ok, I feel bad saying some of this stuff because I know lads like Marcus and that, single mum, they didn't grow up with anything and I was, like, ok. Growing up, like, all my family were in sports. Mum worked for UEFA. And I feel . . . in a way, it's the expectation to earn that? If that makes sense? Like . . .

. . . Like, if we're sharing shit, then. I think one of my fears is not being 'useful'. I . . . I'd hate that.

Harry Kane   . . . Yeah I get that. What Eric says. Being the captain . . .

(*Sighs.*) It's such an honour, I know it is. But you see photos of all the old captains and like –

Eric Dier   You compare.

Harry Kane   Yeah. And I just . . .

Jordan Henderson (*teasing, affectionate*)   You're our captain, Harry.

Dele Alli   You're a wizard, Harry!

Pippa   Look, what we're talking about is trust. And if it feels conditional, on how you well you earn it, or how well you perform. That's not proper *trust*, if you're worried that, by just being yourself, the person will abandon you. Like a teammate, or the fans or –

Marcus Rashford   Or your dad.

Pippa   . . . Exactly, yeah.

A moment. **Marcus** *opens his journal and writes something down*
. . .

The next session.

Gareth   'An *England* team', when we say you're a team, we
don't just mean this one here right now, but that you're part
of this unbreakable chain, a continuum of Englishmen going
back and back and back for more than a century!

(*With his list.*) Harry Kane. Did you know, for example, we've
established that your England legacy number is 1207. That's
your 'place'. Harry Maguire? You're . . . uh, 1223!

They begin lining them up, maybe.

Raheem Sterling   Ah ok, do me, do me.

Gareth   Raheem, number 1190.

Raheem Sterling   Ohmygod that's my pin! . . . Wait, shit,
why did I tell you all that!

Jordan Henderson (*trying to remember it, teasingly.*)   1–1–9–0,
1–1–9–0.

Gareth   That's *your* place in a line, Raheem, that stretches
back to –

*We may see some of these, as memories, in a line curling around and
into the distance, somehow . . .*

Gareth   To, to David Beckham, 1078 . . . to – *me*, even!

Dele Alli/Eric Dier   Whoop! / Yesss, boss.

Gareth   Gareth Southgate, player 1071. All the way back to
. . . Robert Barker. Number – 1. The goalkeeper, Pickers, *for*
England's first international, the first international *ever*
– against Scotland, in 1872. Over a hundred and fifty years,
guys . . . of *stories*.

Flash –

Using our modern **Players**, *we may have snapshots of some infamous England moments from tournaments past, doing as single motifs of moves –*

Michael Owen's great run against Argentina – in France 98 . . .

Paul Gasgoine chipping the ball over a Scottish defender – in Euro 96 . . .

John Barnes slaloming through Brazil – at Euro 84 . . .

Gareth *stares up at these 'memories' as –*

Pippa *with* **Roxanne** *join him.*

Roxanne   Now, you can't put it off anymore, Gareth –

Gareth   Oh God no, please, does it really matter what I wear?

Roxanne   I know you think it's all cosmetic, but these things are an important part of the – 'story'. In the past we've had –

Managers *past appear, modelling their outfit, some 'catwalk' music.*

Sven Göran-Eriksson   A simple, dark, slim-fitted suit, evoking Swedish design simplicity. Clean lines, no nonsense, no fuss. It is about the man underneath.

Fabio Capello   Armani . . . what else? And thick, dark-rimmed spectacles to remind the players that I can see them, right inside them . . . all of them . . .

Graham Taylor   The tracksuit, to suggest you're one of the players. Velour so it's wipe clean, physically imposing and, privately, gives you a fantastic bum.

Gareth   I think . . . I think . . . (*Turning.*) Do – do people still wear waistcoats?

Pippa   Whoow! Look at this! Good luck at the snooker. So. To Russia we go. Training over . . . Remember, we're not in control of every outcome, Gareth. Only our behaviour around it.

Gareth   Yeah. I need to – thank you, remember that. Stay calm.

Pippa   Exactly. Otherwise how will you serve those snacks at flying altitude –

The **Team** *arrive in their suits as the* **Press** *disperse, with the* **Players** *surrounding* **Gareth** *in his new attire, teasing him.*

Raheem Sterling   Yes, bruv! Those threads! You look like one of those old-fashioned, like, gents. Refined, and proper.

Marcus Rashford   That's it! Yes, like an English gentleman.

Gareth   An 'English gentleman'.

Roxanne   Right! Let's capture this touching moment, then it's off to Russia we go!

Gareth   Squad?

Perhaps they race into one last **Team** *photo all together, as we move to . . .*

Scene Five

Russia World Cup, 2018.

A brief sequence – an 'opening ceremony' of the modern-day tournament. As a familiar face appears in the TV studio.

Gary Lineker   Hello, I'm Gary Lineker, and it is great to be back in your homes.

Here, in Russia for the World Cup. And an opener for England, then! Missed this feeling? Maybe you haven't. Low expectations, but high on drama? Let's find out . . .

The scoreboard above reveals itself . . . Tunisia 1–1 England.

Harry Kane *breathing. Calm.*

He takes the free kick and . . . Cheers!

Gary Lineker   Well, there you have it, 2–1. And England win their first tournament opener in over a decade. Bet you didn't expect that at home, did you? And up next for England is Panama. Well, I'm joined now by the Panama Manager, Hernan Dario Gomez. Hernan, you're one of only two men to have managed three different countries at the World Cup. How do you fancy your chances against England?

Panama Manager   The Panama team, we are not worried about England. We hear these stories of what they're up to – modern techniques. Happy clappy, touchy feely. I don't know. But it sounds crazy to me. They have lost their will to win. You can see it.

But then the score appears. England 6–1 Panama.

Gary Lineker   And England are through to the knockout stages then, the final sixteen. But steady yourselves, we haven't won a knockout game since 2006 . . .

Against the black, a whistle goes. And –

Gary Lineker   'That's it. It's penalties. Colombia will fancy there chances, as England remember have never won a World Cup penalty shoot out. Deep breaths everyone . . .'

The group huddle. **Gareth** *here with* **Pippa**, *as well as* **Mike** *and* **Steve**.

Gareth   Ok. You know who's taking them – that's not going to change. You've all chosen where you're shooting. That shouldn't change. Don't turn away from the keeper. Don't listen to the crowd. And whatever happens. You are a team. And you're on the greatest stage on earth, so enjoy it. I am using the word *enjoy*. This is a story, and you are storytellers.

Claps – cheers – a roar.

The penalty shootout between England and Colombia. Sound and light and movement, in a big sequence.

Fans *watching in their respective worlds –* **Gareth** *and* **Pippa** *in the dugout. The England* **Players** *together on the half-way line, as the penalty takers march to the spot.* **Harry Kane** *first . . . as* **Jordan Pickford** *hands him the ball.*

Jordan Pickford   You're a wizard, Harry . . .

Pippa   Breathe. You're breathing . . .

Harry Kane   Harry Kane. 1207.

He shoots, and scores.

He comes back to his team – hugs and slaps.

For Colombia, Cuadrado steps up – and scores.

Marcus Rashford   Marcus. From Wythenshawe. 1215.

He shoots – he scores.

For Colombia, Muriel scores.

Jordan Henderson   Relax, shoulders, neck . . . Henderson. 1170 . . . dad.

He shoots – he . . . misses.

He takes this in – heading back to his **Team***. Who support him, look at him, talk to him . . .*

Gareth   It's ok. They're ok . . .

Colombia's Uribe steps up. He shoots – and hits the crossbar!

Cheers from the England **Players** *and* **Fans***.*

Kieran Trippier *steps up next.*

Kieran Trippier   Trippier. 1222.

And scores.

Colombia's Bacca up next. He shoots –

Jordan Pickford   Jordan Pickford. 1225.

Saves it.

England **Players** *and* **Fans** *going wild. Can't believe it, surely not
. . . as* **Eric Dier** *steps up, as the fifth player.*

Eric Dier   Dier. 1212.

He looks at **Gareth** *and* **Pippa** *. . . He takes his run. He shoots –
He scores.*

Gary Lineker   I don't believe it! England are through to
the quarter-finals. And they did it – on *penalties*! At the World
Cup!

Gareth *performs his iconic celebration to the* **Crowd**. *Something
unleashed. He stands, defiant in the centre. As emanating from the
stands comes a familiar sound . . .*

'It's coming home'.

Blackout.

Act Two

Prologue

Music. The **Team** *march on,* **Gareth** *leading like a marching band's drum major. A hoodeed* **Teenager** *runs to a wall and sprays graffiti:*

'Its Coming Home'.

Fish and Chip Shop Owner (*running on*)   Oy, yer little shit! That's my wall, come here!

Teenager   We love you, Engerland! We do!

Fish and Chip Shop Owner (*grabbing his arm*)   What the hell you doing?!

Teenager   Yeah, PATRIOTIC, innit – *what*?!

Fish and Chip Shop Owner   Look at this mess! It's disgraceful. Where – is the *apostrophe*?! 'I – t – apostrophe – s' – *it is*.

Why? Because It *Is* Coming Home!

As we meet new **Fans** *– a pair of* **Morris Dancers**.

Morris Dancer One   I had a good feeling about these fellas from the start.

Morris Dancer Two   They're a good bunch of lads. You can tell that they care.

Morris Dancer One   I say we're going all the way!

Morris Dancer Two   COME ON ENGLAND!

As they spin into – a song.

Fans *sing from 'Vindaloo' by Fat Les.*

A wedding!

Vicar   Do you, Saskia, promise to love, honour and comfort him, in sickness and in health, for as long as you both shall live?

Bride   I do.

Vicar   And do you accept, as Paul does, in the presence of God, that it is – in fact – coming home?

Bride   I do.

A burst of the national anthem.

A giant flag (maybe?) gets pulled over the **Audience***'s head by two* **Mascots** *running to the stage.*

The House of Commons.

Raucous, braying atmosphere as usual as a **Member of Parliament** *stands for his question.*

Member of Parliament   Mr Speaker, does the prime minister agree with me and the rest of the nation, that football is finally coming home?

Cheers, as **Theresa May** *stands.*

Theresa May   I say to the Honourable Gentleman that I sincerely hope Members across this House will be supporting England as they enter the . . . the quart – . . .

(Checks with someone.) Yes, the quarter-finals in Russia. And that they may even adopt some of that 'can do' spirit to 'push forward' with the Brexit plan currently deadlocked in this Chamber today.

Wedding Guests *sing from 'Vindaloo' by Fat Les.*

England v. Sweden.

We pick out **Pippa** *– watching, slightly removed – during a sequence of the 'two headers'.*

As floodlights hit –

Harry Maguire *leaping/is lifted into the air . . . And we hear the commentary of –*

Guy Mowbray *(recorded)*   'Tossed in towards Harry Maguire!'

And cheers. The **Players** *celebrate.*

Guy Mowbray *(recorded)*

Dele Alli *next – leaping/lifted into the air . . .*

Guy Mowbray *(recorded)*   'Cross comes in. Dele Alliiii! Oh this is the stuff of DREAMS from the Three Lions!'

As we alight – on **Pippa**.

Who, in her own space . . . goes wild. Letting the emotions take over her.

Pippa   . . . YEEESSSS! GO ON, MY SON, GET FUCKING IN!

As the **Players** *celebrate . . .*

Harry Maguire *is being interviewed by* **Alex Scott** *on the sidelines.*

Alex Scott   Harry Maguire!

Harry Maguire   Alex! Look at you. (*To the camera.*) She's crossed over to the other side, boooo!

Alex Scott   Yeah, well, see, there is life after being a player. But this feels like a different England. Fearless, having fun out there.

Gareth   Come on, all of you, over to the fans . . .

Alex Scott   What's going on?!

Harry Maguire   Well that's just the sort of – mental preparations, *mental* side of the game. Sort of what we're all about now.

This moment is crashed by **Jordan Henderson** *and* **Raheem Sterling**, *'photobombing' and rubbing* **Harry**'s *head like it's some sacred artefact.*

Jordan Henderson/Raheem Sterling   Come on! / Have that, will yer!

In the TV studio.

Gary Lineker   Who'd a thought it. Winning on penalties, breezing passed Sweden. Doesn't feel very English, does it? And the euphoric fans here simply won't leave into that Moscow night, singing in full voice . . .

At the wedding, the **Bride** *and* **Groom** *having a drink with the* **Vicar**.

Vicar   First semi-final since Italia 90! I mean where was *that* in the sands? Did that octopus, thing, predict that?

Groom   Octopus?

Bride   Yeah but come on –

Groom   What octopus? *Octopus?*

Bride   Come on, it was the easiest path to the semis for any team ever! Fucking Tunisia?! Fucking Panama?! Fucking –

Vicar   He can't win, can he?! Poor Gareth. Damned if he does, damned if –

Bride   Double the bet, if they beat Croatia; they get to the final then double or quits!

The **Vicar** *and* **Bride** *spit on their respective hands, and shake.*

Vicar/Bride   DEAL!

In the TV studio.

Gary Lineker   Into a World Cup semi-final, then! Blimey the last time that happened *I* was playing, and the grey hairs tell you how long ago that was . . .

Dare we say it, don't get complacent – but a win against Croatia, and it's a final – *final*. As across the land, such scenes we thought had ebbed into distant memory; families spilling out into gardens, amassing in front of big screens in town centres. Together! To watch Gareth's Southgate's great revival of England, risen from the depths – like a kraken!

The more epic and stirring sounds of 'Land of Hope and Glory' begin to sound now, as –

A light picks out an England **Fan** *dressed as an Arthurian knight, sword raised in the air.*

He begins a Mexican wave, as we watch it travel through the projected stadium on screen, fans in the stands continuing it, until it joins back around with our real **Audience** *– who will be encouraged to carry it on.*

Cheers if they do – boos if they don't.

Fans *all gathering to stare up, outwards, at the 'game', full of hope. And then suddenly . . . the music cuts out.*

Everyone looks up at the scoreboard, fading into view . . .

'Croatia 2–1 England' . . .

That's it. Over.

Vicar   . . . Oh I fucking KNEW IT.

The dressing room.

We're only moments after the match. Some **Players** *sit quietly head in their hands. Others pace with pent-up rage.*

Eric Dier *throws something, or kicks his locker. A moment.*

Gareth   . . . Ok. It's natural, all of you, have a moment, it's ok –

Harry Kane   It's *not* fucking ok though is it – sorry, Gareth, that's not at . . . (*To the* **Players**.) But what happened? A goal up and we didn't press guys, / we weren't like –

Eric Dier (*overlapping*)   What happened / at the back, I'm sorry, but –

Harry Maguire   At the back? They never stopped slamming us for about the last – we had no possession at all in midfield –

Gareth Southgate   Ok. (*Looks to* **Phil**.)

Physio Phil   Alright, lads; brutal, three big matches in ten days, I want you ten minutes in the ice bath each.

Gareth Southgate   Pippa.

Pippa   . . . You know, it's natural that we hold onto negative thoughts more than positive ones. For survival, I guess. But . . . we have to consciously fight against that, resist that . . .

Gareth   For now. I want you all to remember . . .We just finished in the *top four*, in the world. And you broke the penalty curse.

You made people proud of their team again. You made *me* proud. So. Yeah, thank you.

Steve   . . . Alright, set to, snap out of it, let's crack on.

The squad are exiting – leaving **Mike** *briefly with* **Gareth**.

Mike   And ok, can I ask 'when', boss? For the post-mortem?

Gareth   When it's just us, Mike.

Mike (*as* **Gareth** *is leaving*)   Right but should we – . . .

But **Gareth***'s heading out, patting some of the departing* **Players**. **Mike** *sighs and goes, leaving just* **Pippa** *loitering with* **Marcus Rashford**. *Sat, solemn.*

Pippa   You ok?

Marcus Rashford   You don't believe in, like, superstitions and all that. Do you?

Pippa (*beat, shrug*)   Well, doesn't matter what I believe, does it?

Marcus Rashford   . . . H doesn't shave, if he's on a scoring streak. Think Eric's been wearing the same socks for 'bout nine years. They know I tap my boots together four times, before a game, but I also, secretly . . . I know it's daft, but I also, like . . . look up, to my nan? And say a couple words, like. Share these big moments, with her, now she's gone. Because of everything she – . . . because she was there.

. . . And, I can't remember if I did that today. With all the . . . I know, I know that's . . . but I didn't play – . . ., I couldn't like impact on the game, when he brought me on late, and I can't remember, if I – and *that's* . . .

He trails. **Pippa** *comes and sits.*

Pippa   Well, that's ok, do it now. I'll do it with you.

Marcus Rashford   Nah, come on, it's all good, I'll be alright.

Pippa   I'd like to.

Marcus Rashford   What (*pointing up*), say something to my nan?

Pippa   Oh, no I just meant, tap our feet.

Marcus Rashford   Oh. (*Then.*) Only it's just sort of like a whole package, you chat and then you tap, and then you –

Pippa   Right, ok. (*Off his look.*) What's her name?

Marcus Rashford   Cillian –

Pippa   Cillian. I'm . . . I wanted to say, your grandson, he was one of the five young men, back against Colombia, who did something for his country no others have ever done.

And that's locked (*clamping her hands*), forever, no one can ever take that away. So . . . Marcus Rashford . . . Yeah and then your feet.

Pippa/Marcus Rashford (*together*)   One-two-three-four –

St George's Park. A post-match analysis with the backroom staff.

Mike   Look, the whole feelgood 'didn't they do well' stuff brings a little tear to my eye as much as anyone's, I'm not completely dead inside, but the fact is they threw away a chance, against a weaker side – of a World Cup final!

Gareth   I don't disagree, so – why?

Steve (*at a board/screen*)   You had Modric and co. able to cut through our midfield, while we just resorted to blasting long balls up the pitch again.

Gareth   That's 'how', I'm wondering why? You're right – they tensed up, they 'hid', again, after we'd finally got them playing free.

Mike   . . . They lacked the 'anger'. Sorry. That 'fuck you, we're gonna crush you fuckers' fire, there was a – a – . . . a 'softness', has crept in, there, somewhere. That's not directed at you, Pippa, your work. Necessarily.

Pippa   A 'softness' – ok. I didn't see that, but, yeah. Some of the fear came back –

Mike   So then tell me what was the point? All that time diverted towards the, the mindset stuff, when it was the mindset that gave in? At the key –

Pippa   It looked to me like they got so far, on the fuel we'd found. The 'penalty dragon' slayed, but after that . . .? They were out of gas. Understandably. It doesn't prove the work was wrong, only that we need to go further –

Mike   D'you know where our focus should be, you know what we have that we didn't have before?

(*Either papers, or digitally.*) Reams and reams of data on our players now. Not just 'renting' them from the clubs anymore, they're *ours*. We know their potential, Gareth – and how to push them. Cause – look, I'm honestly not against it, the 'culture' stuff, but it's become this – out there, this focus on you now, Pippa, for some reason, / wherever that's . . . and –

Pippa   I'm not feeding that – no listen, because that's not what I'm here for. That 'one person changed history' shtick, when we all know it's everyone, feeding in, to create the 'condition' for change. We know that . . .

Gareth   Ok. We draw plans, and it's on to the Euros. 'Act Two'.

Steve   . . . What normally happens in Act Two? Does it get better or worse?

Pippa   I guess we'll find out . . .

Suddenly –

A snap, into –

Theresa May *at her lectern, but also maybe 'post-match' with sports* **Reporters**, *leaning in.*

Theresa May   We gave the British people a choice.

Sadly, I have not been able to implement my vision for that choice. I tried three times. I will shortly leave the job that it has been the honour of my life to hold.

A memory of **Gary Lineker** *from Italia 90 appears.*

Theresa May   I do so with enormous and enduring gratitude to . . .

Gary Lineker *replicates his infamous mouthed reference to Gazza, 'watch him', indicating he's about to cry.*

Theresa May   . . . have had the opportunity . . . (*Crying now.*) . . . to serve the country I love.

She turns to head into Downing Street. But instead – runs to the spot and takes a penalty.

Jordan Pickford *saves it. She sinks to the ground, gutted.*

As flashing blue lights and sirens creep in, some chaos sounds approaching, As everyone begins to cover their face with a mask.

Scene One

Wembley Stadium emerges.

The main setting for this next act. Those old twin towers now a luminescent giant arch. The pitch is empty – desolate – perhaps a groundskeeper pushes a lonely squeaky line-marker.

Gareth *and* **Greg Clarke** *look out from the stands or a box.*

Greg Clarke   Unbelievable, isn't it. Just so – empty and weird. Football actually *is* 'coming home' . . . just not quite in the way we all thought.

Gareth   . . . it's confirmed, then? We're hosting?

Greg Clarke   Postponed, for a year, but yes. That plan they had to share the Euros across Europe this tournament, nice idea, but with Covid? Never gonna happen. UEFA's asked us to pretty much host the lot.

Gareth   . . . Ok. Wow. Ok.

Greg Clarke   A European Championship, at Wembley. Has a familiar ring, ey.

On pitch, a **Younger Gareth** *appears again, on the spot, hands around his neck, looking down.*

Gareth *watches him . . .*

Gareth   . . . Yes, it does. (*Deep breath.*)

Greg Clarke   You know Pelé called it '*the* cathedral of football'. It feels like – something returning. In pilgrimage, or something. Feels right.

And the added expectations that come with that. Not just to 'do well', but – well. To *win*. Here.

Gareth   . . . The hope is always to win, Greg, but – we agreed a timetable, and it's risky, that pressure.

Greg Clarke   I know, but, 'events' and all that.

I'm just asking . . . where that extra juice can be squeezed from. Nice is nice, but winning is winning. Victory over Europe! Unleashing your inner Churchill! Ey, Gareth . . .

Greg Clarke *heads off.* **Gareth** *continues to watch* **Younger Gareth**, *down on the pitch . . . He steps down towards him. Towards the spot . . .*

And strikes an imaginary ball, with 'belief' . . .

In transition to St George's –

The dressing room.

An 'England' flag is displayed, drawn on a flipchart, a digital screen, or hung.

Pippa *is here – but trying to catch up with (and support, if she can) the 'new direction' . . .*

Gareth   This is going to feel different, ok. There *is* such a thing as 'home advantage', sure. But also added focus, and intensity.

And our rivals will be rocking up here, to us, from all over the world. So it would benefit us, I think, as unexpected hosts . . . to have confidence about what 'here' means.

I mean, have we, do we, ever even ask about this? What *is* this? (*At the flag.*)

Jordan Pickford   . . . Is that a trick question?

Gareth   These are going to be everywhere. In every car, millions of homes. And these things can be emotive, and complicated, we know that. Let's uncomplicate it – what do *you* think of, as the place you come from. Or want it to be –

He writes, or projects, the heading 'Your England' on the board.

Bukayo Saka   Wait is this, like, what you do here? You sit around and, like, 'chat'? When's the training start?

Mike (*quietly*)   Good fucking question.

Gareth   This is part of the training, Bukayo.

Bukayo Saka   Yo I don't mind, 'back to school'.

Jordan Pitchford   Ok so what, we just start saying words, do we – England, it's, fucking, the Queen and, cups of tea and –

Harry Maguire   Nowt wrong with a cup of tea, tea's boss.

Jordan Pitchford   I would *never* say owt bad about tea, Harry, I'm just saying! –

Physio Phil   Green and pleasant land etcetera.

Gareth   Exactly, those – that's what I'm saying, but is that *your* England. I . . . I don't come from a, a little cottage near a, a village green, I'm proud that I'm – . . . I'm *Gareth*!

From Crawley. I know that makes me sound like I should be a travel agent. But, for better or worse, I'm England manager. And I fell in love with this game, hitting a ball against my back wall in a small semi in Crawley.

And yes, I just used the word 'love', in a changing room, 'ahh, no'. But come on, gain pride, and strength, from digging into your roots, the real places you come from!

Harry Maguire   Mosborough! South Yorkshire!

Gareth   Yeah, go Mosborough.

Bukayo Saka   Ealing.

Dele Alli   Milton Keynes.

Jordan Pickford   Washington, Tyne and Wear.

Jordan Henderson   Sunderland. Being able to see the ground over the roof tops. Stadium of light.

Marcus Rashford   Absolutely folding people in the streets after school, in Wythenshawe.

Gareth (*writing some down*)   Wythenshawe, exactly, these places that we're told sound like shit places –

Eric Dier   Some of them are shit places – Milton Keynes.

Gareth   – but they're our shit places, they're the fans' places.

Harry Kane   Ah, man, this just made me remember as a kid, in Walthamstow, being upstairs in my room for hours and hours, playing *Championship Manager 01, 02* on Xbox.

Ah, man. They were good times.

A reaction in the room at this memory.

Pippa   Mike? Phil? What about you?

Mike   . . . Uh, well, you know. Sunday league for me, probably, freezing your bollocks off on some run down rec.

Physio Phil   Hearing the *Grandstand* music from the front room, Saturday afternoons.

Jordan Pickford   What's *Grandstand*?

Physio Phil   WHAT'S *GRANDSTAND*?!

Jadon Sancho   Uh, I still go back to the cages I used to play in, in Kennington.

Gareth   Yes, Jadon. Jadon Sancho. 1236.

Physio Phil (*still in disbelief*)   'What's *Grandstand* . . .'

Raheem Sterling   Ok, then, so Jamaica then. What does that mean, uh?

Cause like I hear a lot, that, you know, from some people, that I'm meant to associate bad things, with that flag. But as someone come to north London. I've never had any problem, with it. I like my flag. But it is a thing. To know that some of the people waving it, don't think you should be wearing the shirt. I'm just saying that out loud, that that's all in the mix, in there.

Gareth   . . . Of course. Exactly. Exactly, Raheem, that's all in the mix.

Harry Maguire (*hand up*)   Can I just ask, though.

Gareth   You don't have to put your hand up.

Harry Maguire (*hand down*)   Can I just ask though, boss.

Gareth   And you don't have to call me boss.

Harry Maguire   Ok, so can I ask, Gareth –

Dele Alli   Ohmygod, please just ask it! –

Harry Maguire   I thought 'the past', and the like, the 'weight' of it was the thing we were trying to, like, be 'free' of.

Pippa   But if you know it, it gives you a better chance of owning it. Even – changing it. Like Raheem's saying, we inherit all these symbols and . . . like this place, named after St George. And the three lions on the shirt, that's –

Harry Kane   Yeah why are we 'lions', actually. What is that?

Steve   It's Richard the Lionheart, innit? The Crusades, that was his emblem.

Mike   See, I don't mind all that, it's what we're on, isn't it, a crusade, to bring the 'cup' back home, the Holy Grail etcetera.

Bukayo Saka   A Holy Grail – ni-ice.

Marcus Rashford   But that's also conquering and empire and that stuff. Like, I'll be honest, I didn't know that's what the lions were, on our shirt. That *that's* what they are.

Gareth   What they *were*, Marcus. But for you . . . go out, and represent, as you. Connect, with the fans – as *you*. Your roots, stories, truth. Including . . . social media, if you must –

Bukayo Saka   Ah, yesss. Seriously?!

Gareth   – we can build a more united, supported, environment to play. To . . . win in.

Harry Kane   . . . You think we can win this one?

Gareth   I think we can. I think – we *will*. Right?! We can fucking win this!

A vocal reaction of encouragement.

Harry Kane   . . . But, like, what about the clock, we're stopping the clock?

Gareth   We're aspiring to *beat* the clock, that's all. This work will help, with that pressure. Owning our truths –

Mike   Alongside a more aggressive, tougher training programme to warn you all, following on from Russia we will be stepping the fuck up.

Gareth   Exactly, it all goes hand in hand.

Eric Dier   Right but sorry – you haven't said the answer. (*At the flag.*) 'Our England', why don't you just tell us. Like I'm not being funny but, like, you're the manager, we trust yer. So if you want us to be something, say something, then just tell us, and we'll be it.

Gareth   Guys. *No* . . . It has to come from you. (*Back at the board.*) England – is not a trick question. I promise you . . .

Scene Two

A big sequence of training, social media and 'memories', building and swirling around us, featuring some classic (or modern classic) English songs, peppered throughout . . .

Raheem Sterling   What's up fam. Like a lot of North West London's boy, I grew up in the shadow of the Wembley arch in his garden, taking the bus to school past those gates every day, and now being here, getting ready to play at home, my home, at Wem-ber-ley Stadium for his country . . . my message to you all is: believe.

A training drill led by **Mike** *– tough, brutal, that whips us into –*

Marcus Rashford *is recording.*

Marcus Rashford   My England, growing up . . .? I was actually lucky. Because my mum worked three jobs for her family, sometimes not feeding herself. That's why I set up this foundation. There is so much more work to be done. It's 2021, everyone. Our eyes are open.

Gareth*'s next fashion show, changing his outfit for this new tournament.*

Roxanne   You want to ditch the waistcoat?

Gareth   I want to ditch the waistcoat, yeah; waistcoat's out. It's made me a figurehead, I'm not the figurehead. They are. Something simpler, less fussy?

Roxanne   Polo shirt with light-fitting blazer? –

The transformation begins, watched and egged on by the **Players**, *who now switch to – A Gilbert and Sullivan.*

Players
  For he himself has said it,
  And it's greatly to his credit,
  That he is an Englishman!
  That he is an Englishman!

Harry Kane *uploading his story.*

Harry Kane   Uh . . . Hi. Everyone that follows me. Sorry. We are all working very hard, training together, coming together as a team for Euro 2020. Which, as you know, is actually now in 2021. This year. Which is confusing. But . . .

determined to do you proud. As, as your, your, England captain.

Flicking into –

A brief snatch of the Grandstand *theme maybe –* **Mike**, **Physio Phil** *and* **Roxanne** *doing some snatch of a TikTok dance to it.*

From the TV studio.

Gary Lineker   Whoa, we're gonna 'fake' the crowd noise, if no crowds are allowed in? Is that weird?

Sound Technician   It'll be weirder if we don't, for those watching. Eerie. We've got everything here, fourteen different types of cheers, twelve types of boos –

Gary Lineker   Twelve types of booze . . . I'll have a glass of pinot noir, if you're asking.

As **Gary** *turns to face the camera –*

Gary Lineker   Only three weeks and counting till England opens the Euros. And following their surprise success in Russia, how will Gareth Southgate be coping with these raised expectations?!

The **Players** *launch into a rendition of the Stormzy song 'Crown'.*

Watching all this. **Pippa** *and* **Gareth**.

Pippa   Wow, elite athletes *and* role models now?

Gareth   It takes broad shoulders, to carry a country's dreams. And I need to know who can handle it. For them, more than anything . . .

Pippa   And your voice in all this? Shouldn't you be speaking directly –

Gareth   I don't do social media, Pippa, I'd rather eat my own face.

Pippa   Well. Write to them, then. I dunno, a letter, to everyone. Old school. 'Dear England'.

Gareth *consider this. Stepping away, alone briefly. Trying to find the words, tentatively . . .*

Players
   Heavy is the head that wears the crown –

Gareth   'Dear England . . .'

He rejects this, feeling silly. Into –

– some quickfire questions from the press.

Alex Scott   Not long to D-Day, Gareth, planning any changes to the 2018 squad?

Gareth   I'll be announcing that shortly –

Roe   We have a copy of your updated 'England DNA' philosophy – very academic! Chapter Two is titled 'Who Are We?' Do you really not know who you are, should we be worried?

Gareth   It's really not a philosophy, Roe, just common sense. Excuse me –

*He exits as the **Press** follow, still hurling questions. **Alex** and **Roe** staying behind . . .*

Roe   See, I knew it wouldn't last. This 'great new dawn'? He teases us with access to all the players, now they're just going right over our heads to speak for themselves. We're obsolete!

Alex Scott   Maybe a bridge between them and the fans is no bad thing.

Roe   But their job is essentially a public service role. We have to hold 'em to account. Keep that in mind, yeah?

Alex Scott   I think they just wanna be known as human beings –

Roe   Yeah, or just avoid scrutiny all together. An easy ride!

Alex Scott   . . . Nothing about representing your country is 'easy', Roe. Believe me.

Scene Three

On the training pitch.

Jordan Henderson *privately approaches* **Gareth**, *during this, as he looks over some analytics.*

Jordan Henderson   Gareth? Can I . . .

I have this thought in the back of my head always, that I can't quite shift, about . . .

It was a really special moment, for the team, winning on penalties, in Russia. I know that. And I did feel it – that joy.

I'm just aware that – I was the only one who missed.

You were the only one who missed though, too. Weren't you

Gareth   . . . Yeah, I was, yes

Jordan Henderson   And you don't torment yourself?

Gareth   You're walking proof that a single event doesn't have to define you, Jordan. I believe in you . . . Ok?

Beat. **Jordan Henderson** *nods. And heads off. We stay with* **Gareth** . . . *a moment . . .*

Pippa *watching all this, one step removed now. Concerned?*

As some results 'ping'. And we find –

Dele Alli. *Who enters the dressing room, throwing off his kit in frustration. Hanging up his shirt.*

Pippa *enters carefully, after . . .*

Dele Alli   I thought this whole thing, his-his vibe now was about trust, about trusting, that they've got your back when you're down!

Uuuuhggghhhh! Fuck, man!

Pippa   You've been in your head a lot, Dele, you've a lot going on. I know.

Dele Alli   I'm fine. When I'm playing I'm fine.

Pippa   You're not fine, Dele, and that's why you're not playing.

Dele *looks up at this shirt, hanging up. Despairing.*

Dele Alli   I don't know who that is, man. When I look at that shirt. That name. Alli. I don't speak to those people no more, they're not my family, I went to live somewhere else.

They weren't there for me, and I don't want to be there for them anymore, fuck 'em. No, not fuck 'em, I know they're trying. I just . . . I feel that. Following me on my back.

Pippa   I know.

I had . . . different from you, but I had a lot of that stuff, too, in my house. Growing up . . .

Dele Alli   So how did you become 'you'?

Pippa   How did I become me?

I – . . . I have to work all the time, on being ok. I still make mistakes all the time. All the time.

Dele   . . . Can I not just be 'Dele'? Can you do that? Have just one name? Will they let me?

Pippa   I'm – not sure, but –

Dele Alli   I know that's not really the thing, I *do* know that!

But what's it matter anyways. When you're being dropped.

As **Gareth** *arrives – seeing him.*

Always being dropped . . .

He puts on a different, non-football shirt to leave.

He exits into the light of the tunnel, like **Wayne Rooney** *before him, disappearing. A deflated* **Eric Dier***, sat quietly, clutching his hands.*

Eric Dier   Yeah but . . . *this* tournament. Feels like this tournament – . . .

Gareth   . . . I'm sorry, Eric. There'll be other tournaments.

Eric Dier   Look. If the most use I can be to the team . . . is *not* be in it. Then, that's what I'll do. As my like – duty.

He looks to **Gareth***. Who nods, before maybe looking away.* **Eric** *stands, and makes his walk into the tunnel light . . .*

Pippa   Gareth?

Gareth *sees* **Pippa***. They're alone, in a briefing room.*

Gareth   Pippa?

Pippa   . . . Look, I feel like . . . you're going in this new direction, ok, and that's fine.

Gareth   No, it isn't new, not really –

Pippa   It's your prerogative, a new backroom structure. Fine.

But . . . yeah, I do find it hard. This rhythm. Because . . . essentially my job is to care about them, isn't it. And I do, in the small morsels of time we get before they're off again. Which is hard, but that's the gig, and I will do it, if I'm needed. But if I'm not needed . . .

Gareth   . . . Of course you're needed. Pippa. My God, do we – . . . We just need to also really press forward now, performance –

Pippa   It was always about getting their best possible performance, Gareth. And to sideline the work we agreed to do together, as though it's 'done', like you've completed a video game –

Gareth   It isn't sidelining. Look at them. They learned to be a team – great. Now that team needs to learn to win.

Pippa   'Learn to win'? Gareth, that's not what you need to learn. You have everything you need to be able to win,

Gareth   And yet we *haven't* won, didn't win. And at –

Pippa   In Russia, you proved that –

Gareth   We didn't prove anything, really – what did we prove?!

He paces, forming his thoughts.

That *second* tournament win, still eluding us.

And now here's this chance. The two other times we hosted, '66 and '96, they were – were like 'defining', sort of, chapters, in our . . . and that's on their shoulders. And the best defence –

Pippa   '96?

Gareth   – in the end the best defence they have against the judgement and blame that comes with that, is if they win. And if I ever misled anyone or wasn't clear about that, then . . .

Pippa   You really don't see it, do you. '96, again.

Gareth   Don't patronise me, Pippa. I don't need a therapist to go into all that on my behalf, I've been on that long fucking walk, ok. I know what I did!

Pippa   What '*happened* to you'; not what you 'did', Jesus! And Gareth, I'm sorry . . . you haven't walked away from that spot. You're still there . . .

Gareth   . . .

Pippa   For all your wonderful ability to lead everyone else away from it, in the dressing room and the stands . . . *you* won't leave that spot. Will you.

A moment. **Gareth** *takes a breath. Trying to keep it together.*

Gareth   . . . I keep seeing him. 'Me'. Back turned, head down, hands on his neck, and I try and go to him. To hold his face, in my hands. To tell him it's going to be ok, that this won't define him. But I can't. I can't get to him . . .

Beat. She nods . . . she knows now.

Pippa   I think I should step away, Gareth. Then. I think we're on different paths, want different things. And that's ok –

Gareth   Pippa . . .

Pippa   It's ok.

Turning to go . . . but she wavers.

She goes, leaving him without answering this.

Gareth *steps into . . .*

Harry Kane *alone with him*

Harry Kane   She really left? Pippa?

Gareth   . . Yeah, but, we're all still here. (*Waiting.*) You feeling good, ready? That record's within your reach, Harry – Rooney's record, England's top scorer, think of it –

Harry Kane   Why did you pick me? As captain?

Gareth   . . . Well. You captain your club, you're –

Harry Kane   Yeah but England captain. England captain is . . .

It's like being the Queen, isn't it? It's more than just the job. It's who you are as a person and how that . . . what that *says* about . . .

I'm not great, on 'words'. Communicating. I know people take the piss, about, like . . . my voice, my accent, how I sound and . . .

And people like Hendo and Pickford, they're way more vocal on the pitch.

Gareth   Well. They *scream* and shout, yeah, but. Harry you're carrying something else with you. Like, 'inside' you. Something quieter but people feel . . .

Harry *puts his head in his hands, briefly. The weight of this . . .*

Gareth   Don't be Jordan, don't be Wayne. Don't be like Beckham, or Lineker or Gerrard, be you. Use *your* voice . . .

We move to –

Raheem Sterling *stood on the pitch.*

Abuse and jeers can be heard, directed at him. Cups and beer are being hurled at him.

He stands defiant – as **Harry Kane** *and other* **Players** *rush to surround him, forming a protective wall.*

The dressing room.

Raheem Sterling   What you think it's not the first time I've heard that stuff coming from the stands?

Harry Kane   It's not ok though, is it.

Raheem Sterling   I'm not saying it's ok, I'm saying it's not the first time. Monkey chants and shit, yeah, real original.

Marcus Rashford   And that was a friendly? Yeah, real friendly. What's the tournament gonna be like then, uh?

Gareth   What do you want to do? Should we, us all, collectively, say something

Raheem Sterling   What, just like that, you think it's that easy?

Gareth   No, I'm sorry I didn't mean to make it sound easy.

Marcus Rashford   Everyone will be, like, 'shut up, just play football', they always are –

Raheem Sterling   For me, this stuff happens and we talk about it, and everyone feels good about it, but nothing changes. And today it's, like, oh well, we were playing abroad, abroad that happens, but I'm like – no. No this happens at home too.

Bukayo Saka   Yeah.

Raheem Sterling   But we don't talk about *that*. And I know no one wants to hear *that*.

Jordan Pickford/Harry Kane   I wanta hear about that.

Gareth   And, we can give you whatever back-up, or support you need. As a team.

You all have a right to speak up. We've been giving you these platforms and now . . . if you can use them, to say what you really wanta say. I'll stand alongside you, and speak up too. If that's what you want.

They step into –

A press conference – **McNulty** *and* **Roe** *and* **Alex Scott** *and –*

Raheem Sterling   This is the most important thing at this moment in time, to me. Because this is something that is happening for years and years. Just like the pandemic, there is a disease . . . that we want to find a solution to and stop it.

As the drumbeat of arriving **Fans** *beginning to arrive, over the horizon . . . A sense of the 'tournament' approaching . . .*

And the Wembley arch lights up above us.

Euro 2020 – images and logos . . .

As we shift to **Gareth** *– in his world/his head. The pressure mounting . . . He steps onto the Wembley pitch.*

Back onto that spot. Or circling it, maybe? Beginning to find the worlds . . .

Gareth   Dear England . . .

I can't possibly hope to speak for an entire country, but I would like to share a few things with you, as we begin this journey . . .

It's been an extremely difficult time. It's given us all a new understanding of the fragility of life. In the grand scheme of things, perhaps football doesn't seem so important. And what I want to speak about is much bigger than football . . .

I tell my players that what they are a part of, what we are all a part of, is an experience that lasts in the collective consciousness of our country.

Every game has the potential to create a lifelong memory for an England fan somewhere.

Why do we care so much?

What I know is, what is often forgotten is, how much it means to the players. Players are fans too. The idea that they don't care has become a false narrative.

And we must give them confidence to stand up for their teammates. I have never believed that we should just 'stick to football'.

Of course, I know my players and I will be judged on winning matches. Believe me.

But the reality is that the result is just a small part. It's about how we conduct ourselves. And how we bring people together. That lasts beyond the summer. That lasts forever . . .

The England **Players** *arrive through the tunnel into Wembley.*

Gareth *following.*

As on the pitch, all the **Players** *take a knee . . .*

Some far-off 'booing' begins to grow, and grow . . . As we jump into –

England 1–0 Croatia.

Matt Le Tissier *is with* **Alex Scott**

Alex Scott   Matt Le Tissier, ex-England player, opening game won, 1–0 – but you're not at all enthused by this, are you?

Matt Le Tissier   No, Alex. Southgate's team selection, man, come on. He's just too bloody cautious, timid. When you've got Grealish on the bench, when you've got Foden, these attacking players, why-why-why this defensive, nervous approach, it's infuriating, man.

Alex Scott   But what more does he have to prove – he took us to the semis last time, broke the penalty curse. You are statistically, on record, the greatest penalty taker of all time! – not just England, but anywhere.

Matt Le Tissier   I am. Yeah. I just am. Forty-seven out of forty-eight pens scored.

Alex Scott   Forty-seven out of forty-eight!

Matt Le Tissier   But did he come to me? The . . . the face of 'penalty misses', did he ask me, the 'greatest penalty taker' of all what I think?

Alex Scott   So, what would you say, if he's is listening now?

Matt Le Tissier   Oh, I am sure the woke Mr Southgate won't listen to anything I have to say. I wouldn't be welcome in his – his safe space.

What I will say is this. Real men don't kneel. To win tournaments, you need to display strength. And Gareth, I'm sorry, he's a soft lad in a hard world. I think he should hang his head in shame, what he's doing, bringing his own politics into the sport.

Into –

The sound of 'boos' begin again. As the score is displayed above us – 'England 0–0 Scotland'.

Mike *crashes into a space, with* **Gareth** *and* **Steve** *in tow.*

Mike   FUCK ME. I mean JESUS. Enough, I'm sorry, boss, but that was fucking disgraceful! That's it, it's 'no more mister nice guy' time, seriously. Their heads were who knows where! School fucking meals and activism –

Gareth   I will let them digest and reflect on what just took place –

Mike   Gareth, for fuck's sake! Man up.

A moment.

Steve   Mike, go for a walk.

Mike *takes a breath, and makes to leave before turning back –*

Mike   Do you know something – if we ever do win that fucking 'Best Pussies' trophy, or whatever it's called, 'Fair Play' for going softly-softly, I'll quit. You hear me? I can't stand it –

Steve (*stepping forward*)   Mike –

Mike   You're the one saying call things out, let me call something out then, with permission! Bad things happen! So what? There's floods! Plagues! War! You missed a ball once – ok! We get it! And I'm not surprised, because it was just about the weakest most pathetic strike of a ball I've ever seen –

Steve   Mike, go for a fucking walk.

Mike *bristles and heads off for a breather. A moment between* **Gareth** *and* **Steve** . . .

Gareth   . . . Is it all nonsense, this? Snake oil and fairy dust, be honest, Steve. Doesn't it make a blind bit of difference?

Steve   . . . What? The whole – the 'story' stuff, the . . .?

(*Sighs.*) I dunno, you know me, feet on the ground, stuck in my ways. End of the day, the margin of error, a couple inches this way, few centimetres that, and it all ends up different – why? I . . .

But if *they* believe it. Doesn't matter what I think, about it. Your 'radical' philosophy –

Gareth   Oh – fucking 'philosophy', why do people keep – what's the philosophy, it's just . . . (*Shrugs.*) 'Believe in people.' 'Care about them.' 'Be kind.' There's . . . no philosophy.

Steve   'Caring about people', in sport? And you don't think *that's* radical?

A moment, **Steve** *offering a little smile, before he leaves him alone.*

Gareth *removes his phone, tempted to make a call. He sees . . .* **Pippa** *in her own space, watching him. Waiting. A moment . . . He pockets the phone, and turns into –*

The changing room.

The **Players** *either forlorn, skulking or slamming about. A moment, waiting for* **Gareth** *to speak.*

Gareth   What was it? Do you want me to answer, or do you know?

Harry Kane   . . . We let it get to us. The 'size' of it. I take responsibility for that, like everyone else, we were in our own heads, we weren't a team. And we played with fear.

Gareth   . . . So, what are we going to do?

To –

A briefing room – later.

Captain **Harry Kane** *now has the floor – he's showing the team a black and white video.*

Harry Kane   This is Wembley, old Wembley, the '66 team. The only team to ever win.

We see them, in the memory space, beyond the video perhaps –

The original '66 team of Geoff Hurst and Bobby Moore, in their 'black and white' kits. Perhaps the lights flickering, like an old film reel.

Harry Kane   The final, our only ever final, against Germany.

Geoff Hurst's hat-trick. Peters gets the second. And England win the Cup. Look . . .

Hurst and Moore are dancing with the trophy, along with Nobby Styles.

Harry Maguire   Huh. So goofy, look at 'em.

Harry Kane   Yeah, goofy, they don't care. They're just so happy. 'And Nobby dancing'. From the song. He took his teeth out. His false teeth.

Raheem Sterling   He what?!

Harry Kane   And waved them around. He wasn't in his head about what other people thought. They were all just themselves, even if it wasn't cool. He had no fear.

Jordan Pitchford   So hold on, what, what are you saying?

Harry Kane *puts on some music from his phone.*

Harry Kane   We should dance like Nobby.

Jadon Sancho   Nah, man. What?

Harry Kane   Nobby don't care what anyone thinks. Be like Nobby.

Everyone waits. As **Harry Kane** *begins to dance deliberately cringe and stupidly.*

Bukayo Saka   No, please stop it, I'd rather not win.

Marcus Rashford   That's proper dad dancing!

Harry Kane   Well, I am a dad. So. I don't care – it's only you lot. And you're my brothers.

He continues. **Raheem Sterling** *stands . . . looking unimpressed. A moment . . . Until he begins dancing painfully badly too, going for it.*

Others *join in.*

Out in the stadium.

Gary Lineker   It's the final sixteen, and the fixture that has defined generations. England versus Germany. Here we go again . . .

England 2–0 Germany.

We find – **Harry Kane** *sliding on his knees –*

Gareth *raises his fist to the sky, punching hard. And holds it there, for a moment, almost shaking . . .*

Alex Scott   Gareth! Well, I don't have to remind you the last time England faced Germany in a tournament at Wembley, back in 1996, it ended very differently, but . . . you did it. A new chapter. Are there any words . . .?

Gareth   It's a result that can build belief.

Alex Scott   But given 1996 . . .

Gareth   . . . No I'm just . . . you know.

I was looking up at the screen, and I saw Dave Seaman. And, uh . . . I can't – For my teammates that played with me . . . I can't change that. So it will always hurt.

But – what is lovely is we have given people *another* day to remember.

Alex *places a hand on his shoulder briefly, as* **Gareth** *nods and steps away. Into –*

The drums and the chants return. A new scoreboard overhead: England 4–0 Ukraine.

On the pitch, **Gareth** *hugs* **Jordan Henderson**. *Something unspoken, acknowledged, between them . . .*

Gary Lineker   So victory over Ukraine takes us into the semi-finals! Denmark! I feel like telling these young players, it's not meant to be like this you know. It's meant to be agony! It's meant to hurt . . .

Into –

England 2–0 Denmark.

Gary Lineker   History! In the making! England are in a tournament FINAL! Oh and what new dreams, and old forces, have been unleashed by this team, within the nation?!

Into –

Gareth, *holding his arm and shoulder, heads to –*

Physio Phil's *table.*

Physio Phil   Boss? Alright?

Gareth   This is – embarrassing, but I pulled my arm. Celebrating, something twinged.

Physio Phil   Well. That's what I'm here for.

He taps the table, and **Gareth** *gets up, carefully. As* **Phil** *gently works his arm.*

Gareth   Just getting old, I suppose.

Physio Phil   Nonsense. Should see the muscles the young
'uns pull, delicate as anything.

We might, here, beyond the room, see the **Players** *stretching –
having their limbs and muscles worked on. Almost gentle and
dreamlike, beyond . . .*

Gareth   Doesn't it feel like they're getting younger . . .
Bukayo's eighteen – *eighteen*, which means, oh Christ, I could
just about be his father. Couldn't I. If I'd been a more
confident teenager and had a more adventurous youth.
Which I wasn't, and I didn't.

When did that begin? Other players, coaches, I used to be
like their son, then a younger brother. Then an older
brother, then a cool uncle, then a not-cool uncle, now their
dad . . .

Physio Phil   Yeah . . . (*Working his arm tenderly, softly.*) I did a
stint in the slammer, you know. Made some stupid mistakes
when I was younger, paid for them.

Gareth   . . . Oh. I . . .

Physio Phil   Don't ask. It's not what you go through, in
there, it's what you miss, out here.

That's why it feels the way it feels. Football. These markers,
every four years. It's Italia 90, and you're on a first date.
USA 94, and you're just back from your honeymoon. France
98, and he's taking his first steps . . .

'Time'. And the way it passes. It's about 'time', and what we
do with the bit we have . . .

A moment. He's finished, stepping back.

Physio Phil   Better?

The final.

Steve *and* **Gareth** *in the dugout.*

Steve   Less than ten minutes of extra time, Gareth, still a draw . . .

Gareth? If we're sticking with our five, we need to sub them on, They'll need *some* playing time –

Gareth   We're not at penalties, yet. There's still a chance . . . that . . .

Steve   That what?

Gareth   That it won't go to *penalties*, for . . .

The time ticks down. **Gareth** *pacing, turning . . .*

. . . Ok. Get 'em on.

Steve *raises his hand – whistle blows.*

Marcus Rashford *and* **Jadon Sancho** *are subbed onto the pitch – slaps of encouragement by* **Gareth** *and* **Steve**.

As the final whistle blows.

There's suddenly a dream-like quality to this, not quite real. The audio ethereal and strange.

Gary Lineker   'And there's the whistle. 1–1 to Italy. And that's oh my . . . here we are once more. England's fate will be decided, by penalties . . .'

Through the haze step the five players.

Harry Kane, **Harry Maguire**, **Marcus Rashford**, **Jadon Sancho** *and* **Bukayo Saka**. *Each moving to the spot, one by one* . . .

But **Gareth** *isn't really listening. He's seeing/sensing the emerging* **Mob** . . . *Drums, horns, jeers . . .*

Harry Kane *takes his penalty, and scores . . .*

Harry Maguire *takes his penalty, and scores . . .*

Marcus Rashford *steps up – the* **Mob** *forming around them now* . . .

Marcus Rashford *takes his penalty – and misses.*

Jadon Sancho *steps up, and takes his penalty – and misses.*

Bukayo Saka *steps up, and takes his penalty – and misses . . .*

Gary Lineker   Oohh no! No-o please, the cruelty. Yet again, tears after a penalty shootout for England.

The lights narrowing in on **Gareth**, *isolated and alone.*

Gary Lineker   Players who were asked by Gareth Southgate to step up, despite some of them barely being involved in the game. A huge test . . .

Noise beyond now surrounding and increasingly tormenting **Gareth** *over archive audio and perhaps images of central London being smashed to pieces.*

Pippa *arrives with* **Gareth**, *alone. He smiles to see her . . .*

Pippa   Hi, Gareth.

Gareth   Those boys . . . we put them out there, to face the world, and . . . I think I may have let them down.

Pippa   No . . .

Gareth   I thought I could spare them, but instead . . . Why can't we just win . . .

Fuck . . . FUUUUUUCK!

A moment.

Pippa   You know how to win, Gareth. Whether the stars align, that's beyond you. In my very humble opinion. What England has to learn . . . is how to *lose* . . .

That's what we can control. Who we are when we lose.

The sounds growing again, beyond them. The **Mob** . . .

Gareth   . . . Those old demons. I thought we were changing, but nothing is ever new, is it.

Pippa   How you react to it, Gareth. That can be new.

A moment. **Gareth** *nods. And stands . . .*

A **Hooligan** *appears, a red flare in his hand. And perhaps the unedifying image of the flare up his arse. A new English icon . . .*

As the **Mob** *descends – including the Arthurian knight, as well as* **Reporters** *like* **Roe**, **Matt Le Tissier** *and maybe* **Boris Johnson** *. . .*

Baying for blood, flares as flames, the chants and noise getting louder and louder.

Gareth *leads his team out to face them . . .*

Gareth   DEAR ENGLAND! . . .

The **Mob** *stops. Molotov cocktails and flares hovering in the air . . . waiting . . .*

Gareth   I know you're angry . . . But *please* . . . can you listen . . .

Bukayo Saka *steps forward, reading a note he's written on his phone.*

Bukayo Saka   I have stayed away for a few days, to reflect – calmly – on what happened. This is what we do here now, by the way.

I knew instantly obviously the kinds of messages myself, Marcus and Jadon were going to receive – you have not surprised me.

But despite *these* words I'm saying now, there really are no words to explain how much it hurt, I was hurting, and still am. About the result, and . . .

He looks back to **Gareth** *at this moment.*

Bukayo Saka   . . . And my penalty.

A moment between them . . .

Elsewhere, in the changing room, **Jadon Sancho** *is talking it out with* **Pippa** *and* **Steve**.

And elsewhere, in another room, **Marcus Rashford** *is talking it out with* **Mike**. *Who might put a hand on his shoulder, as he talks . . .*

Bukayo Saka   I'm sorry we couldn't 'bring it home' for you, I am. I know that's a thing. Still a thing . . .

We were three kicks away . . . three kicks, after fifty years, and I know that, and feel like I let you all down.

But life always gives you more chances. Qatar is only months away now, and we *will* be back. So to most of you, majority of you, the majority of England who called out these people . . . we will win.

Love . . . and yeah, I am using that word . . . Love always wins.

Elsewhere, the **Teenager** *from the opening begins spraying new graffiti on his wall . . . By magic, the wall of graffiti reveals itself to be a mural of* **Marcus Rashford**. **Marcus Rashford** *is greeted warmly by* **Fans**, *as he takes it in . . .*

The clock leaps forward to just a few seconds before 'zero' and **Greg Clarke** *steps up to the spot.*

Greg Clarke   'But as chairman of the FA, I regret that I wrongly referred to our Black and ethnic minority players by an outdated and offensive term. Diverse communities in football that I and others – Gareth Southgate in particular – have worked so hard to include. I am therefore resigning from the FA with immediate effect. Thank you.

The clock hits 'zero', as **Greg Clarke** *steps up to take his penalty. He misses.*

The clock then winds back a dozen seconds, to begin a countdown for –

Boris Johnson   As we've seen, at Westminster, the herd instinct is powerful, and when the herd moves, it moves. Thems the breaks. Hasta la vista, baby.

The clock hits 'zero', as **Boris Johnson** *steps up to take his penalty. He misses . . .*

Liz Truss   From my time as prime minister –

Press   FORTY-FIVE DAYS!

Liz Truss   – I know it must appear from the outside that our nation is in a tailspin from which it cannot seem to recover. But it always has. And it always will . . .

The clock hits 'zero', as **Liz Truss** *steps up to take her penalty. She misses . . .*

The **Crowd** *is dispersing now. Leaving a tormented* **Gareth** *alone.*

Then – as if some apparition –

The trophy appears. Glinting, golden. Like some mythical artefact, or prize unlocked.

Gareth *approaches it – maybe reaches out for it – can't grasp hold of it, or doesn't feel able. When –*

Chloe Kelly   WHOOW!

The Lioness snatches it, running around whipping her top off in the iconic image of only a sports bra.

Chloe Kelly   . . . Ha, well . . . Our ladies showed everyone how it's done. We did this on their own terms and this victory is all theirs.

You know, the men, they're always fighting the high expectations. And we suffer just as bad fighting the lows. No one ever expecting anything of us. Well . . . I would like to give a shout out to our coach – Sarina Wiegman!

Sarina Wiegman (*taking it*)   The first trophy since 1966. That's all I have to say to that!

Gareth *joins her in celebration. A hug . . . he means it . . . A snap – they're suddenly alone.*

Gareth   I am so, so happy, for you . . .

Sarina Wiegman   Here, you want to hold it? –

Gareth   No. That's ok, it's yours . . . (*Stepping away.*)

Sarina Wiegman   Sure . . . I mean, I already have one though, with the Netherlands, and a couple others, but –

Gareth   Great, that's great.

A friendly smile between them.

Sarina Wiegman   Must look so simple, other countries; they win then they lose, up then they're down, so they take stock, reset, and reboot. Take stock, reset, reboot. But England? –

Gareth   . . . I tried . . .

I thought that was why *I* was here, what everything was pointing to . . .

Sarina Wiegman   *Your* clock is still ticking, Gareth

Above, the clock ticking down to Qatar reappears, tick, tick, tick.

Sarina *fades.* **Pippa** *returns, who has been watching from her world.*

Pippa   Beginning. Middle . . .

Gareth   . . . And end.

Scene Four

The ticking clock lowers, moving towards its end. **Gareth** *taking it in.*

Qatar 2022 begins. **Gianni Infantino** *arriving – arms outspread.*

Gianni Infantino   It's time. For the Qatar World Cup – 2022!

Stepping into a meeting with –

Gianni Infantino   You know, I don't want to say 'this is all your fault, Gareth Southgate', but I think a lot of this *is* your fault. You turned every player in the world into an activist! And so now what do we do?

Gareth   Sport has never just been about sport, Mr Infantino, ever. That wasn't me –

Gianni Infantino   If Harry Kane wears a 'political armband', of *any* stripes, he will be given a card immediately, at the first whistle. Every other team has agreed; these symbols have *never* been worn, ever – so, it's just you. Just England. We're waiting.

He goes, **Gareth** *left to stew in frustration . . .*

A dressing room.

Steve   Harry, come on. You'll be playing on a yellow card, knowing that one accident, one mistake, and you're out. What that *does*, up there. (*Taps his head.*) You know, all that 'playing with inhibitions', *fear* . . .? Right?

Mike (*pointing to the clock*)   That clock has been ticking down for six fucking years. I can hear it in my fucking sleep. Tick! Tick! TICK! Like the crocodile chasing Captain Fucking Hook, and now –

Harry Kane   Isn't it about leading? Even at a price, isn't it –

Gareth   This is our fault. We shouldn't have put you in that position. The decision's been taken out of your hands, I'm sorry.

Alex Scott *arrives with a microphone to host, making a defiant gesture of slipping on an armband.*

Alex Scott   Here we go, then! Against the controversy and justifiable anger, the sound and fury – England goes again! The final flourish – for Southgate's lions?

The clock continues ticking down, as we blast quickly through some scorelines in graphics –

England 6–2 Iran.

The slightly other-worldly, pandemic recorded cheers.

England 0–0 USA.

And the boos.

Gary Lineker (*joining* **Alex Scott**)   Well, England have got to the quarter-finals in Qatar . . . and all they have to do, to prove they are *finally* a match for World Champions, is beat the reigning ones – France. Can they reach their third semi-final in a row?

We are in –

The dressing room.

A pre-match pep talk, all the **Players** *together.*

Gareth   Ok. Big game, obviously. Perhaps, our biggest. And uh . . .

Remembering **Pippa**. *Perhaps even seeing her – in her own space.*

Gareth   . . . I'm not going to do my normal talk. Actually. You guys are in control now. Ok. Harry? You say some words, this time. It . . . yeah. It's over to you.

He steps away. Letting the team take over.

Harry Kane   Ok, guys. We can DO THIS, right! This is OUR TIME. This is Battle of Waterloo mark II. Right. (*Checking with* **Gareth**.) We won that one, right?

Gareth/Jordan Pickford   We did, yes.

Harry Kane   So believe. I believe in you.

Jordan Pickford   And I believe . . . that Harry's going to
get it in the net twice, and become ENGLAND'S HIGHEST
GOALSCORER OF ALL TIME!

Cheers.

Harry Kane   Maybe . . . cheers. Oh, shit, and . . . one more
practice?

Together (*singing*)   'God save our gracious . . . *king*.'

Harry Maguire   Nailed it.

Harry Kane   And uh, well, look . . . I fucking love you all,
ok. So yeah. (*Claps.*) COME ON, ENGLAND!

All   ENGLAND!

Onto – the pitch.

Gareth *begins his 'long walk', away from all this.*

Harry Kane, *on the spot.* **Gareth** *watches.*

Harry Kane *takes his penalty . . . and it flies over the crossbar . . .
We're fading to . . .*

The dressing room.

Harry *is here, alone.* **Gareth** *joining . . .*

The portable clock still ticking down to the final that will never come.

Gareth *goes over to it, and turns it off. Silence.*

Harry Kane   . . . S-sorry . . .

Gareth   Don't you dare. Harry –

Harry Kane (*in disbelief*)   *Penalties.* I – . . . I thought . . .
There is no plan. Is there? Like, the data, the planning,

Gareth   I think there is, Harry.

Harry Kane   I never miss. I was put here to win. I thought.
Isn't that why *you're* here?

Gareth   I know why I'm here, now. And it's nothing to do with changing what happened to me. We're all defined, by every heartache and lesson and loss. And I wouldn't wipe away any of it. Because I know now, why I am here . . .

Harry Kane *puts his hands around his neck, as* **Gareth** *once did.*

And **Gareth** *goes to him. And removes* **Harry Kane**'s *hands, lifting his head up to face him.*

Gareth   You're going to be ok, Harry. I've got you. You'll be ok . . .

He holds him.

Our other **Players** *are stepping out now . . .*

Harry Maguire   Yeah so basically, obviously we're looking forward to the future now, And so with regards to the manager . . . well, we would just all really like him to stay.

Raheem Sterling   I want to make it clear that I think Gareth Southgate should stay beyond his contract. I know that's not the norm, and everyone has their time, their term. But something is happening, in England. And Gareth is the main reason behind it . . .

Gary Lineker   Well, it's the morning after the night before of a familiar story. And yet, something is different. Nowhere are the burning cars and the broken bottles. Where are the effigies and recriminations? Where is the anger, and the despair? This feels new. Dare I say it . . . this feels like hope . . .

As the **Players** *enter the dressing room where* **Harry Kane** *is still being held by* **Gareth**, *breaking now.*

Jordan Pickford   So . . .when's the Euros? *Where's* the Euros, remind us?

Jordan Henderson   2024. In Germany!

All   Oooh!

Eric Dier   Germany! Dah-dah-dah!

Harry Maguire   Boss, *that's* your third act!

Marcus Rashford   Oohhh, that would be a good story!

Bukayo Saka   That would be a *great* story.

Mike   And guys? (*Holding a trophy up.*) You did win a trophy, you fucking losers. Some silverware, at last . . . the Fair Play Award. Remember . . .? So . . . fair play.

Players   OOOOH!

Marcus Rashford   Oohh, look at this, we're so 'fair'!

Mike   Yeaahhhh, aren't you *nice*, nice boys.

Harry Kane   Guys . . .? . . . I'm really sorry.

A moment. **Rashford** *steps forward . . . to give him a hug. And the others follow.*

Before they begin to rock, weirdly.

Marcus Rashford   Who's doing that?! We're trying to have a moment here!

They break apart, as music fades in, and they begin to do their bad dances, encouraging **Harry** *to do the same – which he eventually does.*

Gareth *watches – clocking* **Pippa**. *In her own space. They acknowledge one another. As the* **Players** *do their stupid dancing.*

Against the backdrop of flashes of World Cups past. Of historic teams, the triumphs and pain. Of mythology and folklore, the sound and the fury

Blackout.

Methuen Drama Modern Plays

include

Bola Agbaje
Edward Albee
Ayad Akhtar
Jean Anouilh
John Arden
Peter Barnes
Sebastian Barry
Clare Barron
Alistair Beaton
Brendan Behan
Edward Bond
William Boyd
Bertolt Brecht
Howard Brenton
Amelia Bullmore
Anthony Burgess
Leo Butler
Jim Cartwright
Lolita Chakrabarti
Caryl Churchill
Lucinda Coxon
Tim Crouch
Shelagh Delaney
Ishy Din
Claire Dowie
David Edgar
David Eldridge
Dario Fo
Michael Frayn
John Godber
James Graham
David Greig
John Guare
Lauren Gunderson
Peter Handke
David Harrower
Jonathan Harvey
Robert Holman
David Ireland
Sarah Kane

Barrie Keeffe
Jasmine Lee-Jones
Anders Lustgarten
Duncan Macmillan
David Mamet
Patrick Marber
Martin McDonagh
Arthur Miller
Alistair McDowall
Tom Murphy
Phyllis Nagy
Anthony Neilson
Peter Nichols
Ben Okri
Joe Orton
Vinay Patel
Joe Penhall
Luigi Pirandello
Stephen Poliakoff
Lucy Prebble
Peter Quilter
Mark Ravenhill
Philip Ridley
Willy Russell
Jackie Sibblies Drury
Sam Shepard
Martin Sherman
Chris Shinn
Wole Soyinka
Simon Stephens
Kae Tempest
Anne Washburn
Laura Wade
Theatre Workshop
Timberlake Wertenbaker
Roy Williams
Snoo Wilson
Frances Ya-Chu Cowhig
Benjamin Zephaniah

For a complete listing of
Methuen Drama titles, visit:
www.bloomsbury.com/drama

Follow us on Twitter and keep up to date
with our news and publications
@MethuenDrama